Jean-Yves Barrier
Architect, Designer, and Artist
2005–2023

Elke Mittmann

Jean-Yves Barrier
Architect, Designer, and Artist
2005–2023

translated into English by
Andrew Ayers

Edition Axel Menges

© 2023 Edition Axel Menges, Stuttgart / London
ISBN 978-3-86905-022-5

Printing and binding: Graspo CZ, a.s., Zlín,
Czech Republic

English version of the original French text:
Andrew Ayers
Design: Axel Menges

Table of contents

1. Jean-Yves Barrier, Piazza XVI Maggio, Ragusa, Sicily, 2012.
2. Jean-Yves Barrier, Saïd Sahbi Mosque, Kairouan, Tunisia, 2018.
3. Jean-Yves Barrier, the city wall of the medina of Sousse, Tunisia, 2018.
4. Poster for »L'Oreille qui voit«, 1974.
5. Stiff Ouessant radar tower. Original sketch by Jean Prouvé, 1978.
6. Sketch by Jean-Yves Barrier for Jean Prouvé.

Introduction

»For me, the architectural work is now identified with these things: there is a street in Seville made up of superimposed balconies, elevated bridges, stairs, noise, and silence, and it seems to recur in all my drawings. Here the search has ended; its object is the architecture it has rediscovered. This rediscovered architecture is part of our civic history. All gratuitous invention is removed: form and function are by now identified in the object; the object, whether part of the country or the city, is a relationship of things. There no longer exists purity of design, which is not also a recompositioning of all this, and in the end the artist can write, in Walter Benjamin's words, ›Therefore I am deformed by connections with everything that surrounds me here.‹ The emergence of relations among things, more than the things themselves, always gives rise to new meanings.«[1]

So wrote Italian architect Aldo Rossi in his 1981 book *A Scientific Autobiography* when describing his conceptual and methodical approach to architecture and his particular view of the city. In this sense, architecture can be understood not as an addition of solitary structures or iconic buildings but as constituting the entirety of the city, something that is intrinsically linked to the history and morphology of the existing urbanity. This *architecture retrouvée* is tied into the strata of history and can be interpreted as being in continuity with the extant city as a sort of »writing«, be it material or immaterial. The morphological, typological, formal, or structural traces that together form a collective memory are what compose the different articulations of this »writing of the city«.

Operating in an intrinsic dialogue with its surroundings, Jean-Yves Barrier's architecture resonates with respect to this reading of the city. His work can never be dissociated from its context, and always seeks to recount the present and future of a place, as though time were the primary condition for architecture to exist. Though architecture is what configures a given space, in Barrier's approach it also possesses the ability to exist in a more global sense at every scale of creation, covering the whole spectrum from the design object to urban form.

Following on from a previous volume, *Jean-Yves Barrier – Architect and Urbanist* (2009), which covered the first 25 years of his career, this book showcases Barrier's œuvre from 2005 until the present, with project descriptions of 25 new realizations. While the initial volume concentrated on the twin orientation of his work as both an architect and urbanist, the current one highlights another facet of his career, namely the interrelation between architecture and art.

A biographical overview

Nothing in Barrier's background predestined him for architecture. In 1966, he enrolled in the architecture section at the School of Fine Arts in Tours, but wanted to become a painter. Two years later he turned his attention to experimental theatre, a discipline he would continue to be involved with until the late 1970s, designing both sets and sound environments with the Théâtre de l'Utopie, as well as co-creating the sequential-art performance »L'Oreille qui voit« (1974) with the poet, author, and dramaturge Pierre Halet (1924–1996). In parallel, he became involved with the Atelier d'urbanisme de l'agglomeration de Tours (Tours Agglomeration Urban Workshop, or ATU), and pursued his calling as an artist, exhibiting his drawings and paintings all over France (Tours, Grenoble, Toulouse, and Monaco, among others) between 1974 and 1980. In 1977, his canvas *Les Javelots migrateurs* represented France at the Madrid Biennale and was acquired that same year by the National Sports Museum in Paris.

Barrier's return to architecture came through art, when in 1977 Halet offered him a plot of land in Chançay (Indre-et-Loire) to build a studio so he could indulge his passion for painting. This first built work, a solar house that adopted ecological principles long before they became the norm, won him an award in the 1979 housing competition organized by the French TV channel Antenne 2 and the French Environment Ministry.

This outline of Barrier's early career underlines the atypical path that led to his becoming an architect. Rather than following the classic curricu-

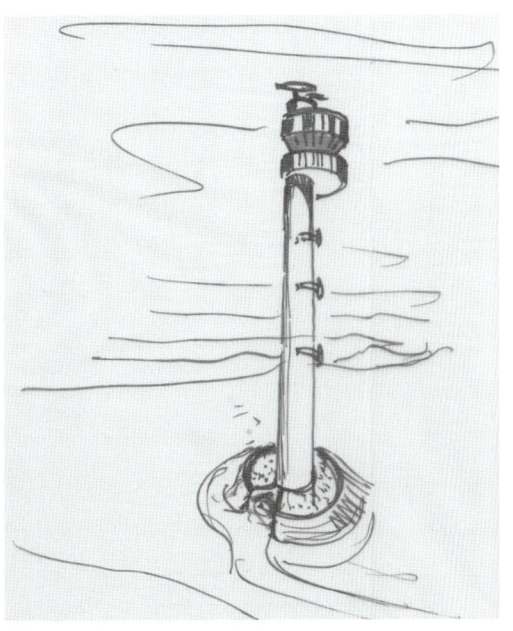

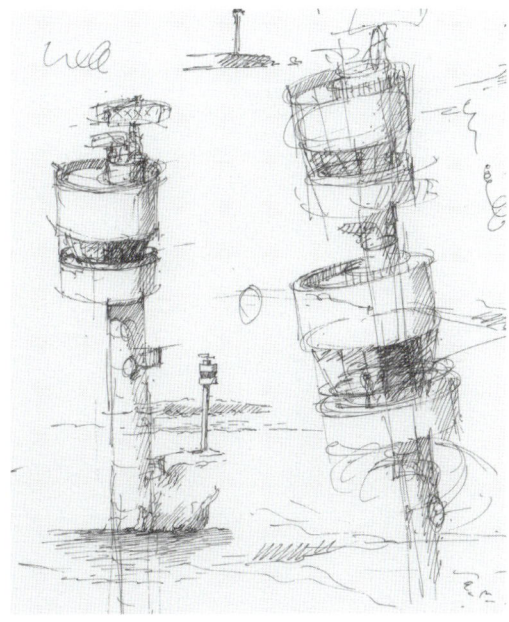

lum, he learnt architecture and urbanism through his involvement with ATU, from 1972 to 1982. At the time, the institution was directed by Jean-Claude Drouin (1933–2020), with whom Barrier realized his first important projects (among them a vacation centre for Radio France in Chançay, 1980–81), and took part in the call for ideas for the development of the eastern and western sectors of the 1989 Paris Universal Exhibition, in particular designing a pavilion for youth and technology (the exhibition was cancelled in 1983 for political reasons).[2] Drouin also introduced Barrier to Jean Prouvé (1901–1984), another major figure in his early career, and in 1978 he had the chance to execute drawings for Prouvé's final work, the Stiff radar tower on the Île d'Ouessant.

Around the same time (1981/82), Barrier took part in a project for the rehabilitation of a disused gasworks in the Tonnellé neighbourhood of Tours. This industrial landmark, with its soaring, 50 m-high reinforced-concrete profile, had been built by the architect Maurice Veillon in 1947–53, but after only ten years' service was closed – France was progressively halting industrial production in favour of natural gas, and by 1969 the plant had been entirely abandoned. Drouin proposed its conversion into an art centre, but it was not until the early 1980s that a firm brief was finally drawn up when the local authority decided to turn it into a centre for arts and technology and a contemporary-art museum, a project that, in 1982, was made part of the programme for the development of artistic creation set up by the then culture minister, Jack Lang. In a series of drawings and sketches, Barrier explored the urban character of this concrete monument, highlighting its silhouette and bringing out its character as a second major landmark in the city of Tours alongside the cathedral.

Following these first projects, which gained wide-scale attention at a national level, and his official recognition as an architect in January 1981, Barrier won the 1983 commission for 27 pieces of railway infrastructure on the new TGV Atlantique line between Paris and Tours. Passing through several protected landscapes, this stretch of track includes Barrier's astonishing Loire crossing at

Vouvray, completed in 1989. Again in 1983, he won a special mention from the jury of *Le Moniteur*'s Prize for a First Work (awarded to young architects for their first building) for his multi-function hall in Chançay. Among the jurors was Renzo Piano, who recognized Barrier's apposite sense of proportions and use of regulating lines, which has proved to be a defining characteristic of his œuvre ever since.

Following these promising débuts, Barrier founded his architecture office in 1985 in Tours. A global approach to architecture and urbanity has always been a defining characteristic of his œuvre: designed for its specific context, his work provides landmarks that allow for a sense of place in rural or suburban settings, while in urban situations his architecture organizes and configures space in such a way as to ensure continuity of the »writing« of the city, in the sense implied by Aldo Rossi. Emblematic of this approach are Barrier's interventions at Saint-Pierre-des-Corps (Indre-et-Loire): winner of the 1988 competition for the redevelopment of the town centre, he designed a major ensemble comprising a municipal library, a social and cultural centre, and a concert hall and auditorium. Completed in 1996, the complex is currently the subject of a bid for historic-monument status. In the same period, Barrier extended Saint-Pierre's Line-Porcher school, which won him a nomination for the 1991 Équerre d'argent (France's most prestigious architecture prize), and he would later design the layout of Saint-Pierre's Avenue Jean-Bonnin (2000).

While developing his ideas of an »urban architecture«, Barrier was also experimenting with the possibilities of domotics, in particular at his own home in Chambray-lès-Tours (Indre-et-Loire, 1988–90), where all the electrical systems are connected to a central computer and can be programmed via remote control or by Internet. The house was also an experiment in new ways of living, featuring a »sound« or »communication« space, designed for watching films and listening to music in ideal conditions, and a »health space« next to the bathroom that is fitted out with balneotherapy equipment and a large glazed bay that

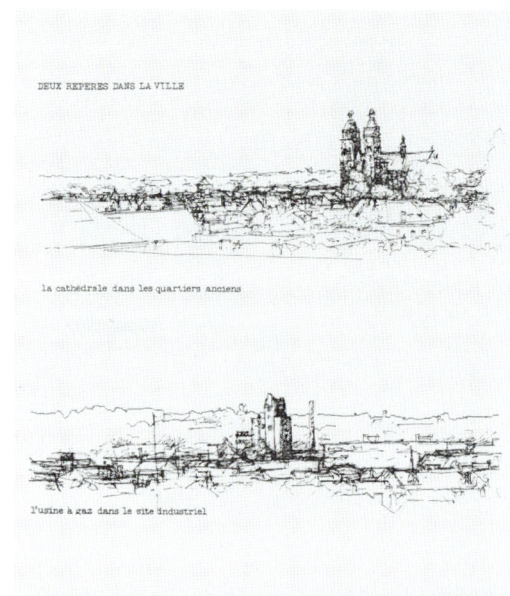

7. Multi-purpose hall and fire brigade garage in Chançay, 1983.
8, 9. Project to transform the gasworks into a centre for scientific and technical culture, Tours. Sketch and model. Atelier d'urbanisme, 1982.
10. Extension of the École Line Porcher, Saint-Pierre-des-Corps, 1990/91.
11. Saint-Pierre-des-Corps festival hall, 1993.
12. Avenue Jean Bonnin, Saint-Pierre-des-Corps, 1994–99.
13. Carrefour de l'Hippodrome, Chambray-lès-Tours, 1988/89.

allows sunlight to pour in. Bioclimatic principles also guided the house's design, with north–south orientation, a timber frame, and abundant glass, thereby ensuring plentiful daylight and a sense of warmth.

As of the early 1990s, Barrier's œuvre began to include artistic interventions that sought to bring a new identity to public spaces. Among them were the Carrefour de l'Hippodrome in Chambray-lès-Tours, which won him the 1993 »Ruban d'or« (Gold Ribbon), awarded by the Ministère de l'Équipement, des Transports et du Tourisme, or his project for the street-lighting of Saint-Pierre-des-Corps, which earned him the 1995 »Ville Phare« national prize from the Académie nationale des arts de la rue.

Also in 1993, he met the American architect Peter Eisenman (born in 1932) in the context of an international competition for a new centre for contemporary creation in Tours. As his architect of record,[3] Barrier discovered Eisenman's work, which at the time was concerned with notions of deconstruction, fragmentation, fractal geometry, and folding.

Since the late 1990s, Barrier has worked extensively on housing, building his first ensemble of dwellings in Paris (Bercy) in 1993–96 and a series of houses in Rennes as well as the Amirauté apartment building (1996–2000). Rennes is also home to his extraordinary Salvatierra block, which in 2004 earned him the Habitat solaire, habitat d'aujourd'hui (contemporary solar dwelling) award from Observ'ER (the Observatoire des énergies renouvelables, or Observatory for Renewable Energy). Realized as part of the European Commission's CEPHEUS programme (Cost Efficient Passive House as European Standard), which was launched in 2004 to build, evaluate, and promote low-energy housing prototypes, Salvatierra stood out through its use of ecological materials. Realized with a lean reinforced-concrete frame, the building is clad in blocks of cob – a mixture of earth and straw – that ensure stable temperatures thanks to their high thermal inertia.

Barrier has also won awards for the shopping centres he has built in heritage areas, for example Blanc Carroi at the edge of Chinon, which earned him the 2008 trophy in the eighth national competition for the best Entrée de ville (town entry), awarded by the Ligue urbaine et rurale (Urban and Rural League), or the 2010 trophy for the creation of business and commercial parks awarded by the CNCC (Conseil national des centres commerciaux, or National Council for Shopping Centres). That same year he completed another emblematic project in Chinon, the »vertical link«, an urban elevator that connects the lower and upper towns, thereby redefining this sector of old Chinon, dominated by its royal castle, by setting up a surprising dialogue with the historic fabric.

Barrier's search for a dialogue with context does not only apply to the built heritage but also to topography and other geographic specificities, as is the case for a certain number of projects he realized in Saint-Pierre-des-Corps, among them housing in a flood-prone zone.[4] His structural and architectural solutions at Les Jardins Boileau (2010–13) and the Maison Lunais were hailed at a national level when they were listed in the Environment and Housing Ministries' 2016 Grand Prix d'aménagement (development prize), whose theme that year was »How to build better in flood-prone construction zones«. In 2019, Cap 55, an office building in Saint-Pierre-des-Corps, won the Pyramide d'argent (silver pyramid), awarded by the Fédération des promoteurs immobiliers de France (FPI, or Federation of French Real-Estate Developers).

This brief overview of Barrier's career, which mentions but a small part of his output since the 1970s, shows all the structural and architectural inventiveness of his work, as well as the extraordinary variety of typologies to which he has turned his attention over the years.

An œuvre of diversity

»Producing an architecture for today means working within the paradigms of our epoch«, says Barrier with respect to his way of thinking and designing. In this constant effort to reflect the Zeitgeist, his approach, whatever the typology or context – detached homes, collective housing, social dwell-

ings, public facilities, urban developments, or utilitarian structures such as supermarkets, employment offices, or engineering infrastructure – is never repetitive or doctrinaire, but allows him the liberty to produce innovative solutions for each project. On the other hand, a careful reading of the territory and the context – be it from the point of view of landscape, urbanism, or architecture – allows him to reinterpret what are often complex historical situations, using his observations to invent or update an architecture that seeks to dialogue with its surroundings with a view to bringing out the best in them. Barrier also strives to renew the coherence of the urban situations in which he intervenes, be they town centres, abandoned industrial sites, or loosely developed peripheral zones, which he redefines and rehabilitates through typologies such as contemporary garden cities (Les Brandons in Blainville-sur-Orne (Calvados, 2000–07)), or the compact and dense housing ensembles he built at the Papeteries de Bretagne redevelopment site (Rennes, 2006–13).

Not only do architecture and urbanism fuse in Barrier's approach, he also connects art, design, and architecture according to a method and a way of thinking that allow every scale to be coherently tackled, uniting several disciplines in the same work. Among his recent realizations, the most emblematic example of this transdisciplinary approach is his 2016–19 youth hostel in Tours, where he was given full rein to combine art, design, and architecture in one project: the interior décor, the furniture, the objects, and the building itself are all indissociably linked. Meanwhile, other projects, such as his interventions in public space or the landscape, are located at the border between land art and artwork *tout court*, as demonstrated by the *Coqueplicots* on the Carrefour de l'Hippodrome in Chambray-lès-Tours (2015–17), an updating of a project initially realized in the late 1980s. Moreover, the *Coqueplicots* harks back to Barrier's first experiences in the world of theatre, since it literally stage-manages the loose urban periphery in which it is located, a place that was devoid of urban cues from which to draw.

EISENMAN ARCHITECTS, 40 W 25TH ST, NEW YORK, NY 10010 TEL 212/6451400 FAX 212/6450726

6 FEB 94
DEAR JEAN YVES

I WAS SAD TO HEAR THE RESULTS OF THE COMPETITION, HOWEVER, I THINK IT WAS BETTER TO LOSE NOW, THAN TO LOSE LATER. FIRST, I THINK WE HAD A GOOD PROJECT, SO WINNING OR LOSING IS OF LITTLE IMPORT. SECOND, WE MET AND AGT TO WORK TOGETHER, AND THIS WAS USEFUL, IF NOT FOR NOW, LATER.
FINALLY, I WANT YOU TO UNDERSTAND MY FEELING ABOUT THE MODEL. IT IS A MATTER OF PRINCIPLE THAT I DO NOT WANT IT EXHIBITED. FIRST, WE WERE NOT GOOD ENOUGH TO WIN, SECOND THEY WOULD NOT ADMIT IT INTO THE JURY. I DO NOT WANT TO GRACE THEIR EXHIBITION WITH IT.
I TRUST WE WILL HAVE THE OPPORTUNITY TO WORK AGAIN. FOR NOW, MY BEST REGARDS.

It can be said that Barrier's œuvre contains the idea of an *architecture retrouvée*, in the sense that each project seeks to go back to architecture's universal foundations. Form or image are secondary concerns to Barrier, his primary interest being architecture's essential principles, which he reinterprets with multiple variations in each of his projects, using a lexicon of constants that seems to define the very essence of each realization.

Regulating lines – the quest for perfect proportions

A recurring feature in Barrier's methodological lexicon is the search for perfect harmonies through the use of regulating lines. In this quest for balanced proportions, the whole is united with the parts, since he seeks to create harmonic relationships between each component of the building. This approach has a long history going back to classical antiquity, where regulating lines governed the proportions of temples (e.g. the Temple of Po-

seidon in Paestum, 430 BCE), and continued into the Romanesque era (the Abbey of Saint-Étienne de Marmoutier, 11th century CE), the Gothic period (Cologne Cathedral), the Renaissance (Alberti's Palazzo Rucellai in Florence, c. 1455, or Palladio's Villa Foscari in the Veneto, c. 1560) and on into the 17th century (François Blondel's Porte Saint-Denis in Paris, 1671–73), not to mention in Ottoman mosques or Hindu temples, to give just a few emblematic examples. While regulating lines regained a certain importance in the 19th century, particularly in the ideas of Frenchman Auguste Choisy (1841–1909) and German architect August Thiersch (1843–1917), it was in the early 20th century that they would be introduced into Modern architecture by Le Corbusier (e.g. the Villa Stein de Monzie, Garches, 1927).

As a method, regulating lines are based in the use of triangles and rectangles to determine the proportions of a building. »The regulating line is a satisfaction of a spiritual order that leads to the pursuit of ingenious and harmonious relations. It confers on the work the quality of eurythmy«, wrote Le Corbusier in 1923.[5] This approach, which moreover seeks to establish a cadence and rhythm in the built work, is one of the oldest systems of architectural design, and it could be said that to a certain degree Barrier connects the entirety of his œuvre to this rich history, and in doing so links each of his buildings to the very origins of architecture. Numbers, geometries, and measurements are for him the tools that allow regulating lines to be established, with units, halves, thirds, quarters, fifths, and the golden section coming together to create arithmetical relationships that create a harmony of proportions. Such an approach allows all the parts of a building to be related both to each other and to the whole, as well as establishing a proportional relationship between the building and its surroundings. The result of this geometric »exercise«, which Barrier renews with each project, is perfect visual cohesion.

To put it another way, Barrier's mastery of proportions allows him to objectify the forms he produces. In this sense, form is not the starting point for the creative act, but the consequence of many factors, among them the search for a harmony of proportions, which often leads him to the simplest geometric form, as can be seen in many of his schemes, among them the industrial kitchen in Rennes (1994–96) or his recent design for a Leclerc supermarket in Fondettes (Indre-et-Loire).

The fold – a form of resistance

Another constant in Barrier's work is the fold, which he uses both geometrically and structurally. In the second half of the 20th century, and in particular the 1980s and 1990s, the fold became a recurring architectural feature all around the world, used, for example, by Walter Netsch at the United States (Saudi Arabia, 1999). But it was above all Peter Eisenman who, as of the 1990s, developed an architectural approach to the fold based on the philosophical concepts set forth by Gilles Deleuze.[6] In Eisenman's approach, folding became a system of spatial differentiation linked to

themes of continuity and infinite formal variation, with repetitive operations of folding giving rise to singular formal results.

Even though Barrier worked with Eisenman in 1992/93, at a time when the American architect was experimenting with and developing his idea of the fold in architecture (as can be seen in their competition entry for the Centre de création contemporaine Tours, he uses folding as a structural, regulating, and formal device. Eisenman, on the other hand, uses the geometric form of the grid as the departure point for the act of folding, a method akin to a conceptual protocol established at the beginning of the design process.

For Barrier, folding is a way to manipulate solid matter and dissolve mass into lightness, the fold creating internal tensions of traction and compression that allow a reduction in envelope thickness. A vector of weightlessness, the fold also produces a sense of movement that dynamizes and diversifies the façade, giving it both a coherent image and its own, recognisable identity. He first used the approach in 1993 at the library in Saint-Pierre-des-Corps, where the folding of the upper windows allows better light penetration, all the while accentuating the structural aspect of this ring of glazing.

Not merely an architectural form in Barrier's œuvre, the fold is in fact a fundamental, transversal tool for designing at every scale. This globality of the fold in his work can be seen in particular as of 2008, when he began producing design objects that allowed him to explore the relationship between art and architecture. In 2010 he launched the wall-shelf range Tol'Pli and the Tol'Rigami lamp, which he followed in 2012 with Bi'Pli, an ingenious modular system of folded sheet-metal book ends that slot into horizontal slabs to form freestanding shelves. His experiments with folding also allowed him to generate artworks such as his *Nomad* sculpture, shown in the 2015 »Archi-Sculpture« exhibition at the Villa Datris, a contemporary sculpture centre in L'Isle-sur-la-Sorgue (Vaucluse). Barrier has also used folding in inte-

19. Study sketch of a building complex, 2019.
20. Study sketch for a graphic work, 2019.
21. Tol'Rigami lamp, 2010.
22. Rotonde of the municipal library of Saint-Pierre-des-Corps, 1993.
23. Leclerc de Fondettes shopping centre, Fondettes, 2015/16.

[1] Aldo Rossi, *A Scientific Autobiography*, Opposi-tions Books, 1981, p.19.

[2] With this new World's Fair, which was an-nounced in 1981 with the theme »The paths of freedom: a project for the third millennium«, France was planning to remodel the banks of the Seine in Paris to celebrate both the bicentenary of the French Revolution and the centenary of the 1889 Exposition Universelle. See Denis Fainsilber, »Quand la France torpillait son Exposition univer-selle«, *Les Échos*, 5 March 2016, https://www. lesechos.fr/2016/03/quand-la-france-torpillait-son-exposition-universelle-204379

[3] Among those taking part were COOP Himmel-b(l)au, Claude Parent, Rem Koolhaas, Daniel Li-beskind, and Peter Eisenman.

[4] Saint-Pierre-des-Corps is located on a sand bar between the Rivers Loire and Cher, and is at high risk of flooding.

[5] Le Corbusier, *Towards a New Architecture*, 1923.

[6] See Gilles Deleuze, *Le pli. Leibniz et le baroque*, Éditions de Minuit, Paris, 1988.

[7] Karl Bötticher, *Lehre der tektonischen Grund-formen. Dorische, ionische und korinthische Bau-weise*, Berlin, 1874, p. 5.

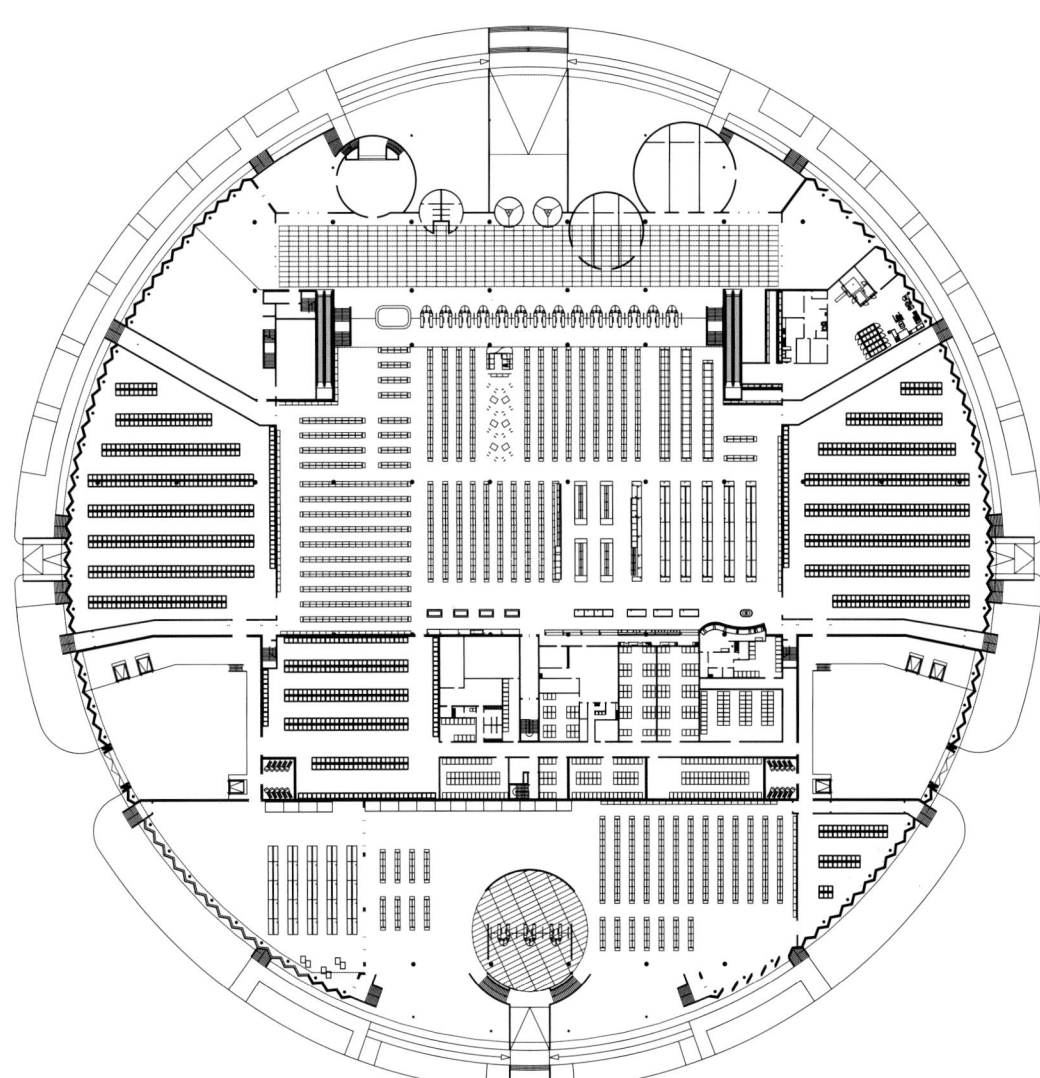

rior design, such as in the monumental staircase at the Audilab HQ in Saint-Pierre-des-Corps (2017 to 2021), which features the installation of *7/7* made up of folded disks suspended from the ceil-ing, and in his work in public space, such as the 552 *Coqueplicots* he installed on the Carrefour de l'Hippodrome in Chambray-lès-Tours.

While the fold, thanks to its modularity and repetitive capacity, occupies a transversal position that embraces every scale of creation in Barrier's œuvre, it is also inherently linked to the structural approach in his architecture, the goal being to make visible the structural logic of each project, all the while ensuring an economy of means. This logic leads, in turn, to another constant in his work, namely the rational use of materials and tex-tures for their intrinsic properties. The specific ma-teriality of Barrier's buildings is highlighted in a me-thodical approach that leads to the final architec-tural form. One could go so far as to quote the German architect Karl Bötticher, who in 1874 wrote that »knowledge of the structural logic of a material allows understanding of the different parts of the building, its form, and the organization of its space«.[7] To describe the capacity materials, have to generate and configure architectural space and form, Bötticher used the term *Tektonik* (tectonics), which refers not only to the word's »constructive« meaning (according to its Greek et-ymology) or its geological use, but is the origin of another way of understanding architecture that

one might define as »form follows tectonics«. Even if Bötticher's theoretical ideas might at first seem rather far from Barrier's general preoccupa-tions, they are in fact central to them, because the intrinsic properties of materials and their structural logic are a major component in his architectural design process.

All the approaches described above, be it the desire to continue the writing of the city, the re-course to regulating lines, the use of folds, or a »realist« attitude towards materials and structure combine in Barrier's design process, literally »con-densing« in each of his projects, thereby demon-strating that for him architecture is not about cre-ating forms or beautiful images but a methodical process that, through these constants, allows a new architectural solution to be found for each given programme. In this sense, Barrier's multi-faceted œuvre is entirely unique, and resists all attempts at classification.

Headquarters for the *Ouest France* editorial team, Île de Nantes, Nantes, Loire-Atlantique, 2006–08

Located in the waters of the Loire in central Nantes, the Île de Nantes (originally several smaller islands) has been the site of a vast urban-regeneration operation since the 1990s. After a proc- ess of deindustrialization saw its shipbuilding activities cease in the 1980s, the city began planning the cultural recovery of this abandoned heritage, setting out to transform the island into a new neigh- bourhood while preserving the memory of its mar-itime and industrial past.

In the late 1990s, based on a careful reading of the terrain, the architects/landscape designers Alexandre Chemetoff and Jean-Louis Berthomieu drew up a masterplan for the island that sought an urban diversity in which »everything is possible«. A first »landmark« came in 2000 with the building of Jean Nouvel's new courthouse, after which the construction on the very same quayside of Jean-Yves Barrier's headquarters for *Ouest France*, in 2006–08, marked a second major step in the Île de Nantes regeneration scheme.

The programme is divided between two buildings separated into three distinct volumes. The first building houses the *Ouest France* group's editorial team in offices of 3,200 m², while the second, the 5,300 m² Le Rhuys, which was acquired by Mado France, contains office space for: the Nantes teams of Radio France (France Bleu Loire Océan); the Ministry of Justice (the commercial court and district judges); the headquarters of Samoa (the Société d'aménagement de la métropole ouest-atlantique de l'Île de Nantes); and *Moniteur Ouest*. In this way, a true media hub has been created, bringing together press, radio and television under one roof.

In their masterplan, Chemetoff and Berthomieu sought both to make the quayside publicly accessible and to create new thoroughfares that would open up views and perspectives onto the Loire. Barrier's project fully takes on board these ideas of placemaking. To open up views towards the river, he traced out a thoroughfare that would become the principal axis of the project, with the main parts of the complex located on either side. Wedge-shaped in plan, Le Rhuys develops horizontally oriented façades on both the river front and along almost the entire length of this new street. The *Ouest France* wing, meanwhile, more vertical and compact, acts as an urban marker on the river, but also develops accommodation behind, thereby defining the other side of the new thoroughfare and making of it a true urban street. Even if the latter physically separates the two structures, it is also what unifies them, by creating a continuous line between their bases, which anchor them to the ground.

This »common base« between the two main volumes gives way to a more complex dialogue above, inherited from classic Modernism, where a tension between verticals and horizontals brings about a sensation of harmony and balance: for each horizontal there is always a corresponding vertical. This principle is also reflected in the way the two façades are structured: the quasi-dematerialization of the first three floors of the *Ouest France* building – thanks to the dynamic and almost frenetic rhythm of its close-spaced, vertical-ly oriented windows, which are incorporated into a folded building envelope – is matched by the three floors of Le Rhuys whose fenestration is slower in rhythm and more widely spaced, as well as being set flush with the envelope, resulting in a flat and almost monolithic surface. The third volume, a prolongation of Le Rhuys, exhibits an even more pronounced dematerialization, because the concrete structure becomes a »façade« thanks to its twelve giant square bays.

This desire to achieve balance is also found in the way the building is integrated into its immediate environment, since the three-part vertical façade division (base, standard floors, roof) of a neighbouring 19th-century building is reproduced in the elevations of the adjacent *Ouest France* block: a base, a central section and an attic floor repeat this cadence of urban verticality, the string courses of the existing edifice continuing naturally into the new volumes. As in all of Barrier's buildings, the architecture has been carefully designed so that perfectly drawn lines anchor the whole as a tightly controlled mass in the urban context.

From the outside envelope to the interior spaces, the desire to design every detail by hand in an almost Miesian spirit – the shutter boxes, the solar-panel structure on the roof, the layout and proportions of modules, the vents, cables, etc. – forms a sort of »invisible« layer that creates a harmonious and well-proportioned relationship between each part and each detail. Perhaps the most interesting thing to point out here is that all this complexity was already present in the first sketch for the project, drawn up in October 2002: elevations, proportions, the general morphology and the choice of colours. But the project isn't just the result of formal or functional considerations, for it is also the metaphorical transposition of the image of a newspaper: the black volumes correspond to printing ink while the concertinaed façades evoke the folded paper of a broadsheet.

While this kind of balancing act is a constant in Barrier's œuvre, the *Ouest France* building stands out in the subtle handling of light and materials as well as in the search for a structural solution that is unique to each project. Here, the waterside site led him to respond to the river's changing light and the reflections from its surface. A dialogue with this environment begins structurally, thanks to the vast glazed openings that allow maximum river views while framing the architectural and urban panorama of the opposite bank in an almost photographic manner. Where materials and construction are concerned, the *Ouest France* wing enjoys particularly luminous interiors thanks to the use of Danpalon, a polycarbonate that reflects the river's sparkling colours by day but at night is translucent, turning the structure into a giant magic lantern that finds itself with an abstract double reflected in the Loire. The effect is reinforced by the fact that the polycarbonate is corrugated, thereby multiplying the almost prismatic reflections of the light and helping to make the ensemble a strong presence in the cityscape – a landmark and perhaps even a contemporary monument in this new neighbourhood of Nantes.

1. Main façade facing the Loire.
2. Site plan.

pp.16, 17
3, 4. Exterior views.
5. Stub road between the two parts of the property.

14

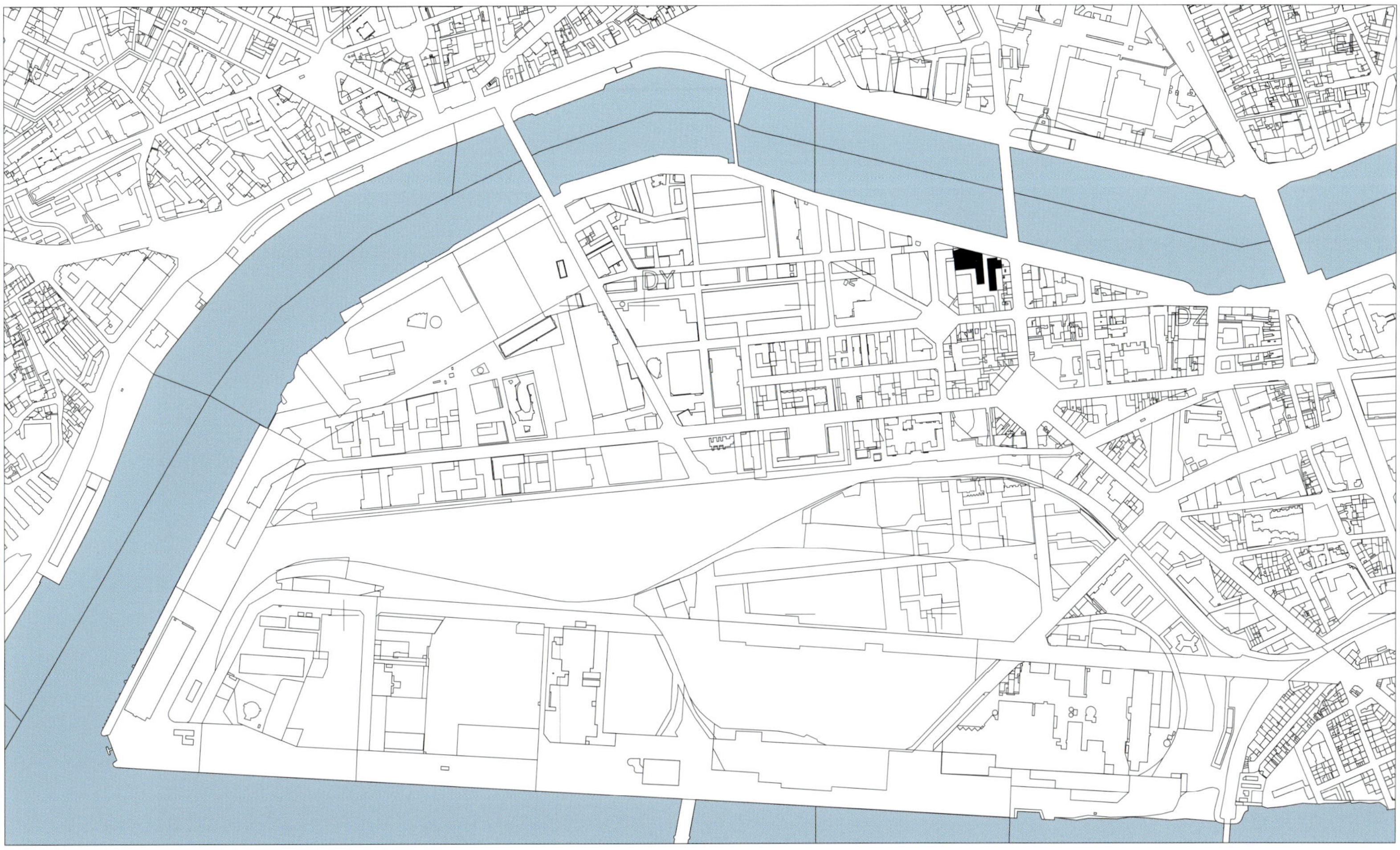

Blanc Carroi shopping centre, Chinon, Indre-et-Loire, 2007–14

Located in the La Plaine Des Vaux redevelopment sector, between the old town of Chinon and the Chinonaise Forest, the Blanc Carroi shopping centre is home to a Leclerc hypermarket, a Brico-marché hardware store, various other small and medium-sized retail spaces, as well as a petrol station and a drive-in restaurant. It is situated within the perimeter established by UNESCO in 2000 when it declared the Val de Loire a World Heritage Site. As a result, the architectural approach seeks to merge this retail zone into the surrounding landscape by evoking a clearing in the forest, with abundant light at the centre and shadow at the edges, close to the trees.

Among other recommendations, UNESCO prohibited large commercial signs and billboards, which reinforced the idea of integrating them completely into the façade so that they would »disappear« when seen from afar and »reappear« as you move closer – an ambiguous approach to advertising that makes it an integral part of the architecture. Going beyond the paradigms and new archetypes of the »decorated« shed and the »duck«, as theorized by the architects Denise Scott Brown and Robert Venturi in the 1970s with respect to emerging typologies of retail construction, the Blanc Carroi shopping centre proposes a new approach that plays on different scales of vision, billboards and other forms of advertising becoming purely architectural features. This is achieved using a double façade into which the billboard is entirely integrated, allowing it to appear in a »filtered« manner, like a watermark, thanks to polycarbonate panels and a grid structure with huge expanses of glazing. There is a certain abstraction

in the result, as though the billboard is partly disconnected from its advertising function. All along the façade, a succession of advertising panels can be read in different ways depending whether they are seen from a moving car or from the point of view of the pedestrian. The choice of colours – black for the building's base and translucent polycarbonate for the upper part – recalls the contrast between the light-hued stone and the dark slate traditionally used for construction in the region.

The shopping centre's three parts are linked by a roundabout. On each side we find a building with an adjoining car park, planned on a perfect grid, thereby expressing a search for neutrality and abstraction in the structuring of the plan and the design of the buildings. Moreover, the grid helps to compensate for the sloping ground, and is highlighted by certain architectural features, such as the metal drain pipes, which also visually balance this change in level by establishing a continuous, abstract building line across space.

The grid structures not only the plan but also the rest of the architecture, in particular the arcades. This internal street, which links the different buildings, makes the grid manifest via a series of repeating metal columns. As in most of Barrier's projects, metal is not used in a purely structural or technical way, since it is also an integral part of the architectural design. Here it takes on a tectonic aspect: the structure needs no cladding but instead generates an elegance and lightness of form, as well as a texture and a volume – in other words, structure becomes architecture in a Miesian sense, the one indivisible from the other.

The Blanc Carroi shopping centre was awarded the 2010 trophy in the eighth Concours National des Entrées de Ville.

1. Site plan.
2. Double façades protecting the walkway.
3. The walkway.

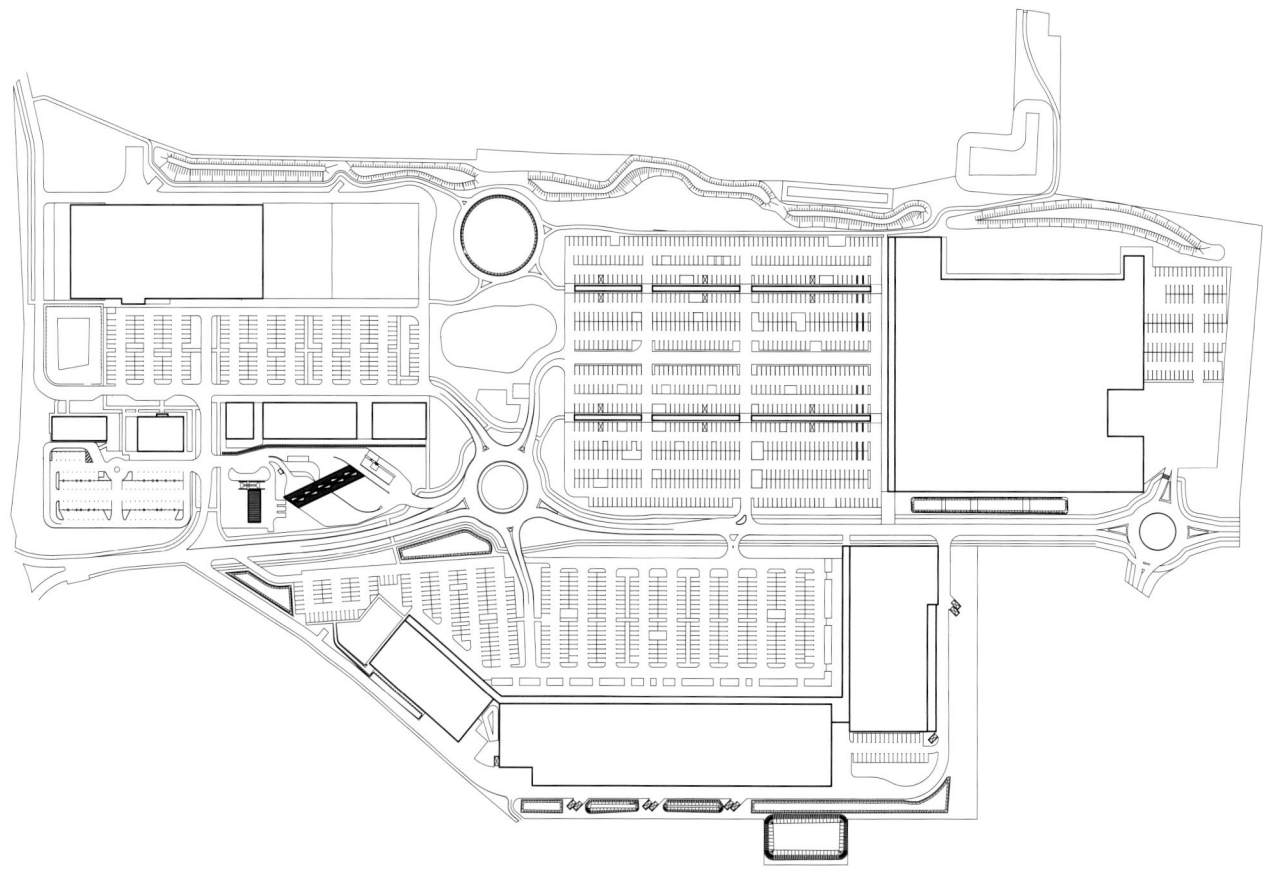

4, 5. Service station.

Leclerc de Fondettes shopping centre, Fondettes, Indre-et-Loire, 2015/16, project

In 2015, looking to expand, the Centre Leclerc in Fondettes decided to construct a new building at the northern edge of the *commune*, near a residential neighbourhood, on a plot of land located between a light-industrial zone and the site of future large amenities. This new shopping centre will provide 5,000 m² of retail space as well as all the infrastructure needed for logistics, delivery and parking. The main entrance will be sited in the axis of the large roundabout that leads into Fondettes, and all the shops will face towards the historic centre. Meanwhile, at the building's rear, there will be a landscaped park with rainwater-retention pools.

Given the lack of a pertinent architectural context, and because of the shopping centre's size, visibility and impact on the environment, the goal was to create a new landmark, an urban sign, a monument even. In reaction to these parameters, Barrier opted for a simple, autonomous form, a perfect circle with a simple curved façade, which will allow all the shopping centre's activities to be contained in one single volume – circulation, storage, service courtyards, technical spaces and everything else needed to ensure the functioning of a large commercial outfit.

The circular form is highly unusual for this kind of programme, which is usually housed in a simple rectangular box, demonstrating that the architectural choice does not simply follow a functional flow chart but determines the organization of the interior and its relationship to the exterior. This is manifest in the plan, reminiscent of an electronic circuit board, the circle becoming a sort of »spatial discipline« that governs technical functioning and the flow of goods and people round the centre. Not only formal and functional, this choice is also ecological, since the 2016 ALUR law stipulates that building footprints must be kept to a minimum to prevent urban sprawl. As a result, 80 % of the parking will be located in the basement.

The perfect circle also recalls an urban archetype, the fortified village, which was hermetically sealed against the exterior and concentrated a multitude of activities inside. All of the shops and retail space, but also all the infrastructure (escalators, travellators and footbridges), as well as the administrative spaces with their patios and relaxation areas, constitute, just like the medieval village, an »urban settlement«.

Even if treated as an envelope wrapped round the building, the façade isn't simply a membrane separating outside from in, but, as always in Barrier's work, is carefully detailed. Thanks to its dynamic folding, the elevation vibrates, the alternating solids and voids thus created offering different views and sources of light. Planned in white aluminium (Myral), the building will mark its context with its pure architectonic force, becoming an image unto itself and doing away with the need for billboards and signs to tell you what it is.

The Centre Leclerc in Fondettes is closely linked to another of Barrier's retail realizations, the Blanc Carroi in Chinon. Once again, he continues to experiment with a new generation of supermarkets by inventing an architectural language for a typology that hitherto has generally been entirely lacking in architectural merit – a paradox when you think about it, for why eschew an architectural and urban approach where thousands of people can appreciate it every day?

1–4. Elevations.
5. Computer-generated perspective of the building façade.
6, 7. Plans of the semi-buried car park and the ground floor.

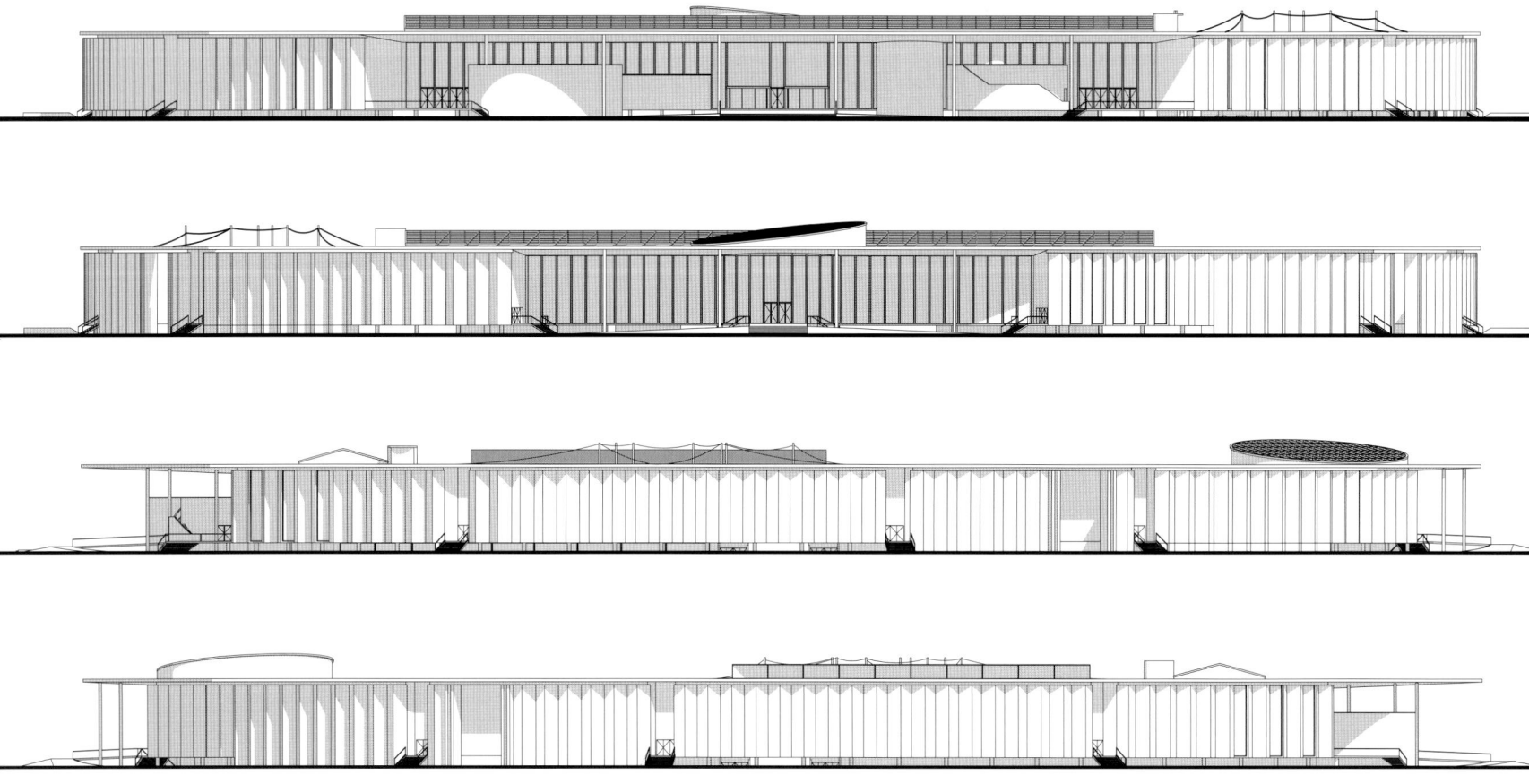

Architecte: Jean-Yves Barrier   © AnImage 3D

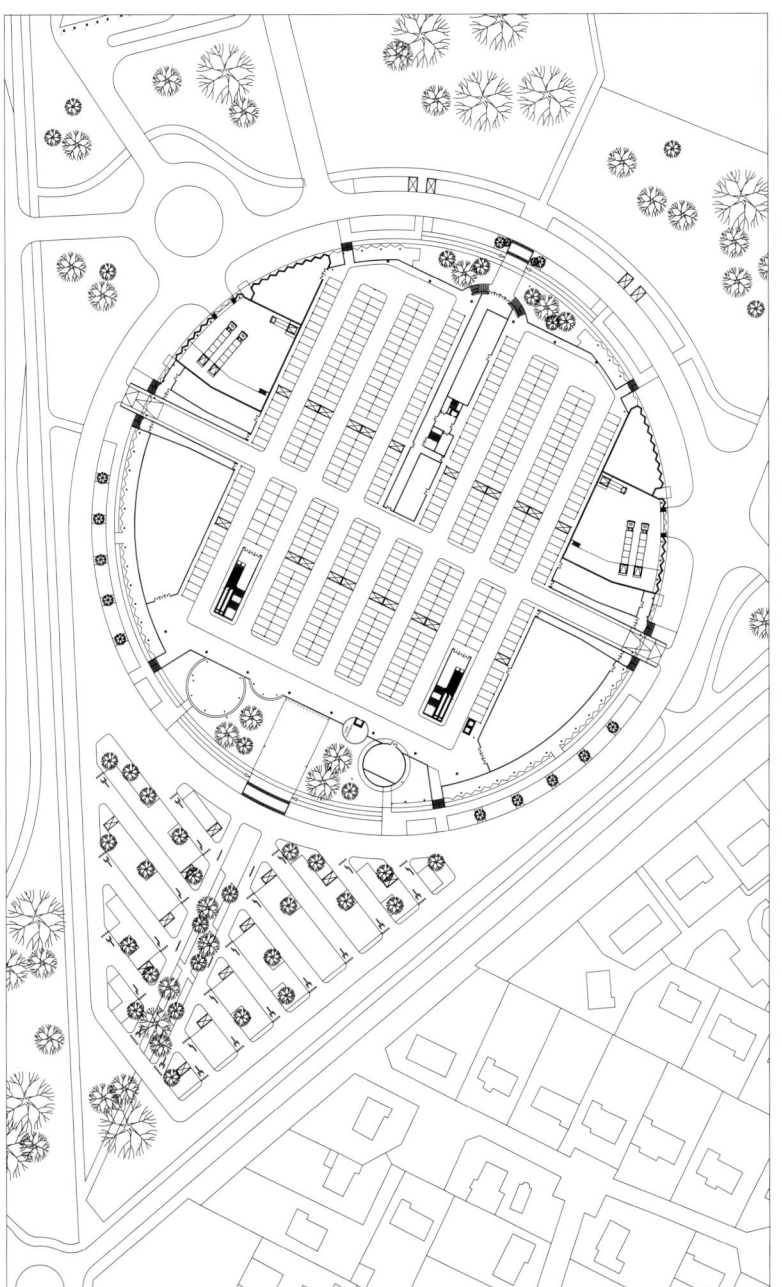

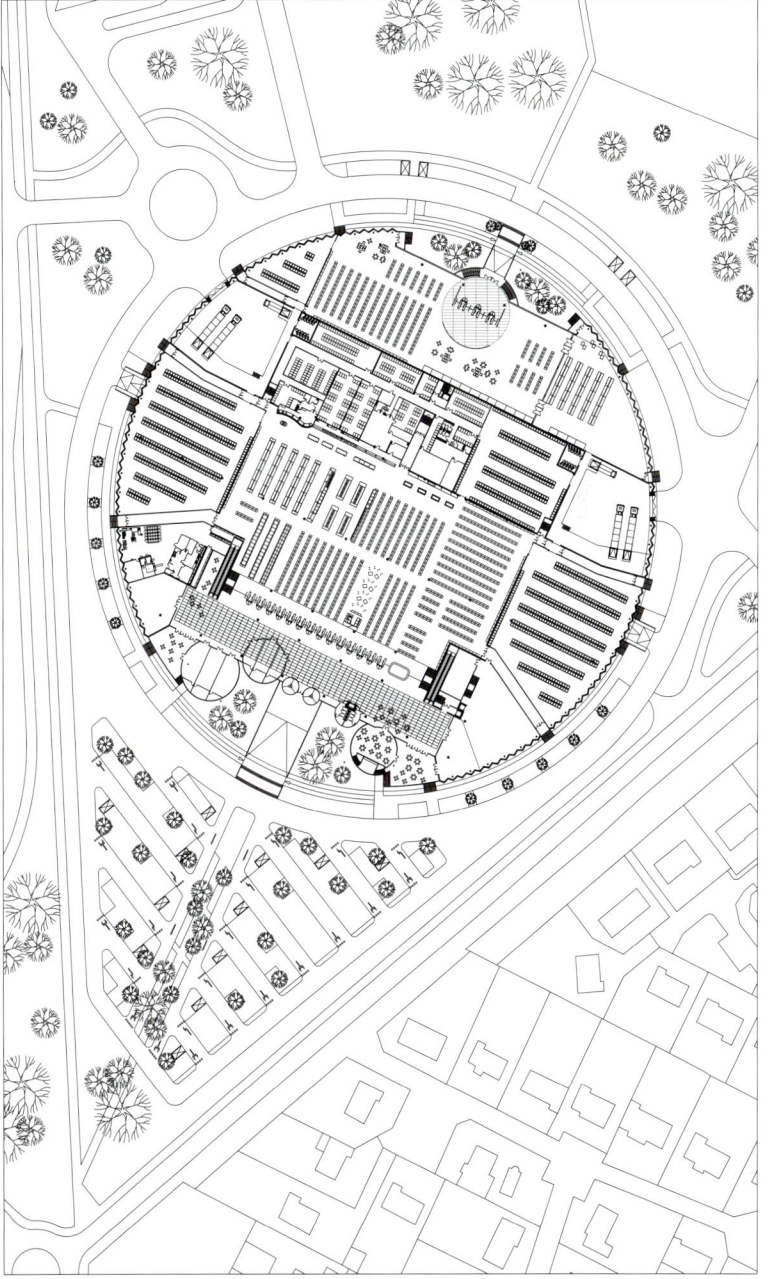

Orangery at the botanical garden in Tours, Indre-et-Loire, 2006–09

Created thanks to the tenacity and generosity of the pharmacist Jean-Anthyme Margueron (1771–1858), the botanical garden in Tours is located on former wetlands crossed by the Sainte-Anne stream. The original project included a school of botany for students at the new school of medicine and pharmacy just opposite. Laid out between 1831 and 1843, the garden has remained exactly as initially intended, apart from the arrival of glasshouses, in 1869, and the evolution of its collections in the years since. Today the garden has a double status, linked to its scientific origins: the municipality looks after maintenance, while the University Laboratory of Vegetal Biology at the UFR of Pharmaceutical Sciences is in charge of research. Landmarked on the supplementary inventory of French national heritage, the site was designated a »Botanical Garden of France and Francophone Countries« in 2000.

In 2007–08, the decision was taken to extend the garden by 6,500 m² to the north, with a new orangery, a building for the gardeners and a contemporary garden, baptized »des deux mondes« (»the Garden of the Two Worlds«). The construction of the new orangery, as well as the renovation of the original glasshouses, was undertaken in order to conserve endangered species from South Africa and the tropics and for overwintering non-hardy plants. The new glasshouse, which measures around 1,000 m², is placed next to a tall central stone building with a historicizing décor, either side of which are the lower historic greenhouses in glass and metal; backing up like a buttress against the northern wall of the historic structures, the 47 m-long, 10 m-high addition seeks the light by rising several metres above them, but without dominating. Conceived for overwintering large plants in tubs that are sensitive to the cold, such as bougainvilleas and olive, orange and palm trees, the orangery, with its frank, taut lines, doubles up as an exhibition space during the warmer months.

By evoking the archetypal form of the 19th-century greenhouse, dematerialized through the use of glass, the new orangery sets off and amplifies the historic structure. Though inspired by the classic model developed as of the late 17th century, which became particularly common in the 19th century thanks to the industrial revolution (when technical advances made it possible to construct vast buildings in iron and glass to overwinter fragile plants), Barrier's realization, also in metal and glass, is far more sophisticated with respect to climate control, offering the ideal environment for plant growth. Both a receptacle and a living organism that reacts to external climate, the new orangery provides specific conditions of light, temperature and hygrometry thanks to roof-mounted sensors that feed a computer controlling the blinds and windows, which open or close depending on temperature and the amount of sunlight. Developed in partnership with the botanists so as to best stabilize the parameters, the system makes the building autonomous. Also in the classic greenhouse tradition, a maintenance footbridge crowns the edifice.

Even if the building seems high-tech where its functioning is concerned, it is nonetheless a work of architecture that stands out due to its lightness (despite its great volume) and the lean, balanced design of its metal structure. The latter derives from Barrier's concern to treat each material in such a way as to reveal all its intrinsic qualities and its authenticity (an approach for which the engineer Jean Prouvé was famous); bringing out the intelligence of the material, Barrier has created not just a constructive system, but a work of architecture in which each piece is designed individually to create a harmonious ensemble. The regular, repetitive rhythm »magnifies« the archetypal form of the greenhouse and turns this giant rectangle into a backdrop for the Jardin des deux mondes.

But the orangery doesn't only enter into dialogue with the historic greenhouses, it also responds to a second new structure, which forms the other focal point of the botanical garden's extension: the gardeners' building, located in the axis of the greenhouses. This second contemporary structure helps make clear the switch from the old garden to the new as the visitor passes from one century to another.

Responding to the orangery's simple volume, the rectangular (11 x 19 m) building dialogues with the orangery's all-glass exterior by proposing a different form of lightness: a façade in perforated aluminium that filters the view from the inside and is printed on the outside with a photograph of a bamboo grove. In this way, a certain intimacy is obtained by completely enveloping the building like a membrane. While the orangery transposes the archetype of the historic greenhouse, the gardeners' building looks to the far more ancient form of the rural Mediterranean house with its central patio, the latter not only bringing daylight into the heart of the interior but also providing a relaxation space for the gardeners. Another garden is perched on top of the roof and, when lit up at night, seems to float like a discreet evocation of the labour that goes into ensuring the botanical garden will survive for future generations.

The existing structures were renovated by Barrier's office in tandem with construction of the new orangery.

1. Site plan with the park.
2. View of the greenhouse from the park.
3. Axonometric view of the greenhouse.

pp. 26, 27.
4. View of the greenhouse from the street.
5. Existing part of the greenhouse.
6, 7. The gardeners' house.

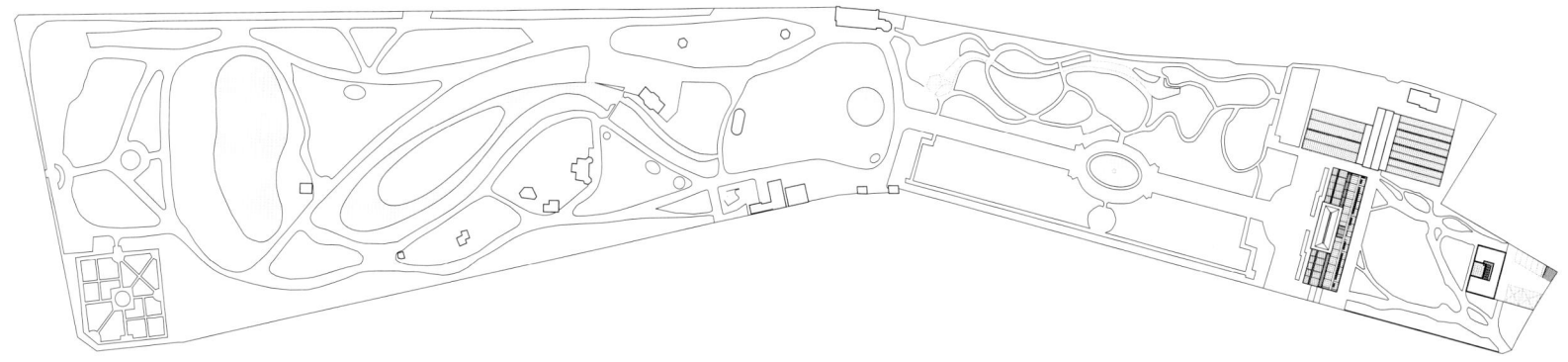

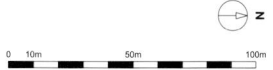

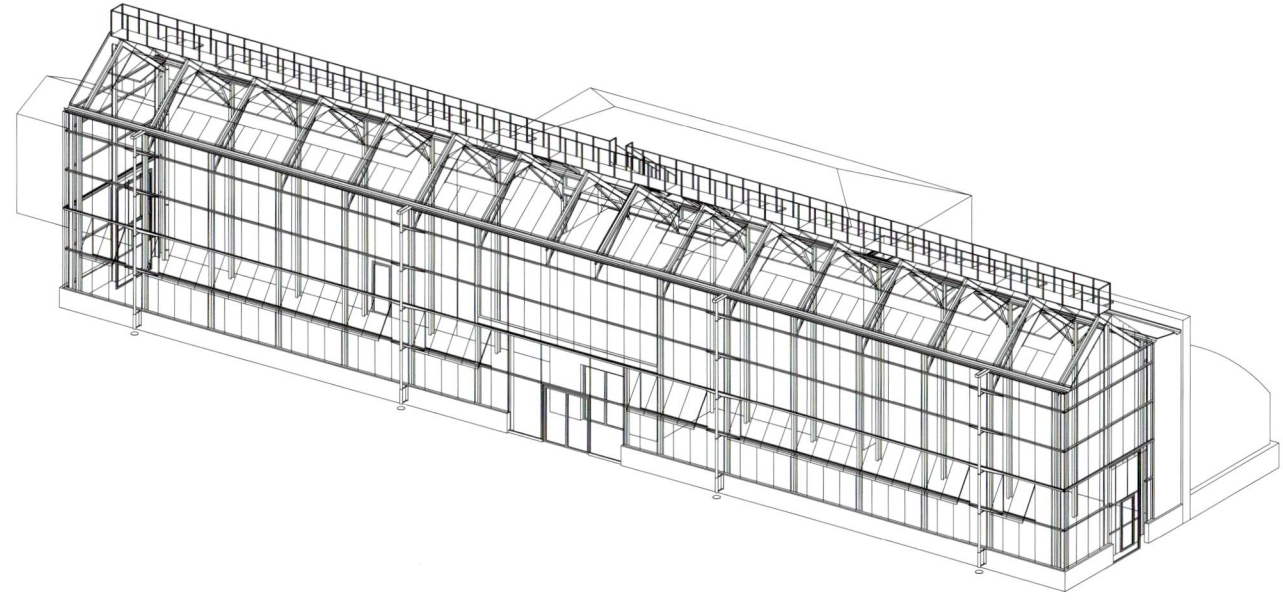

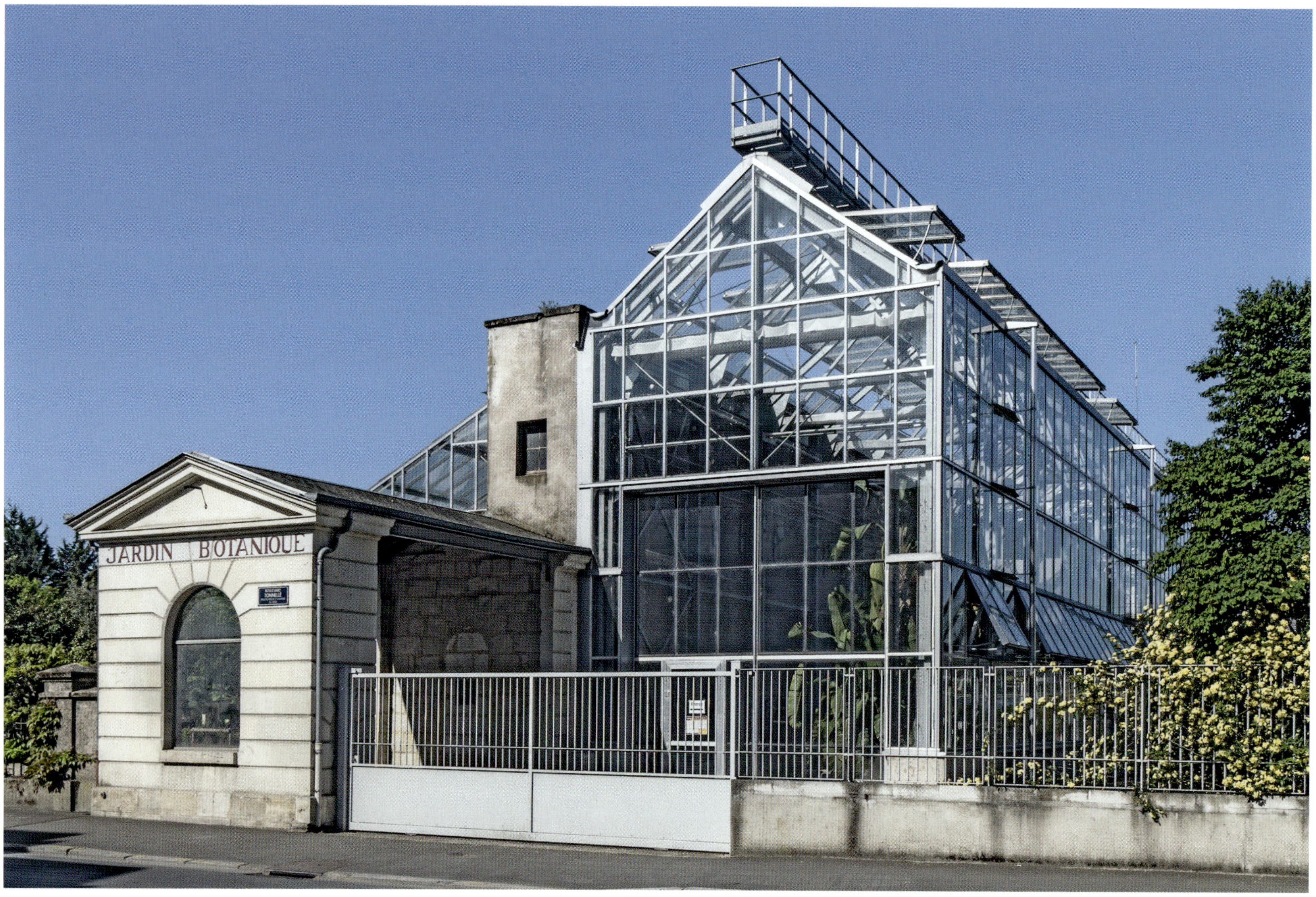
JARDIN BOTANIQUE

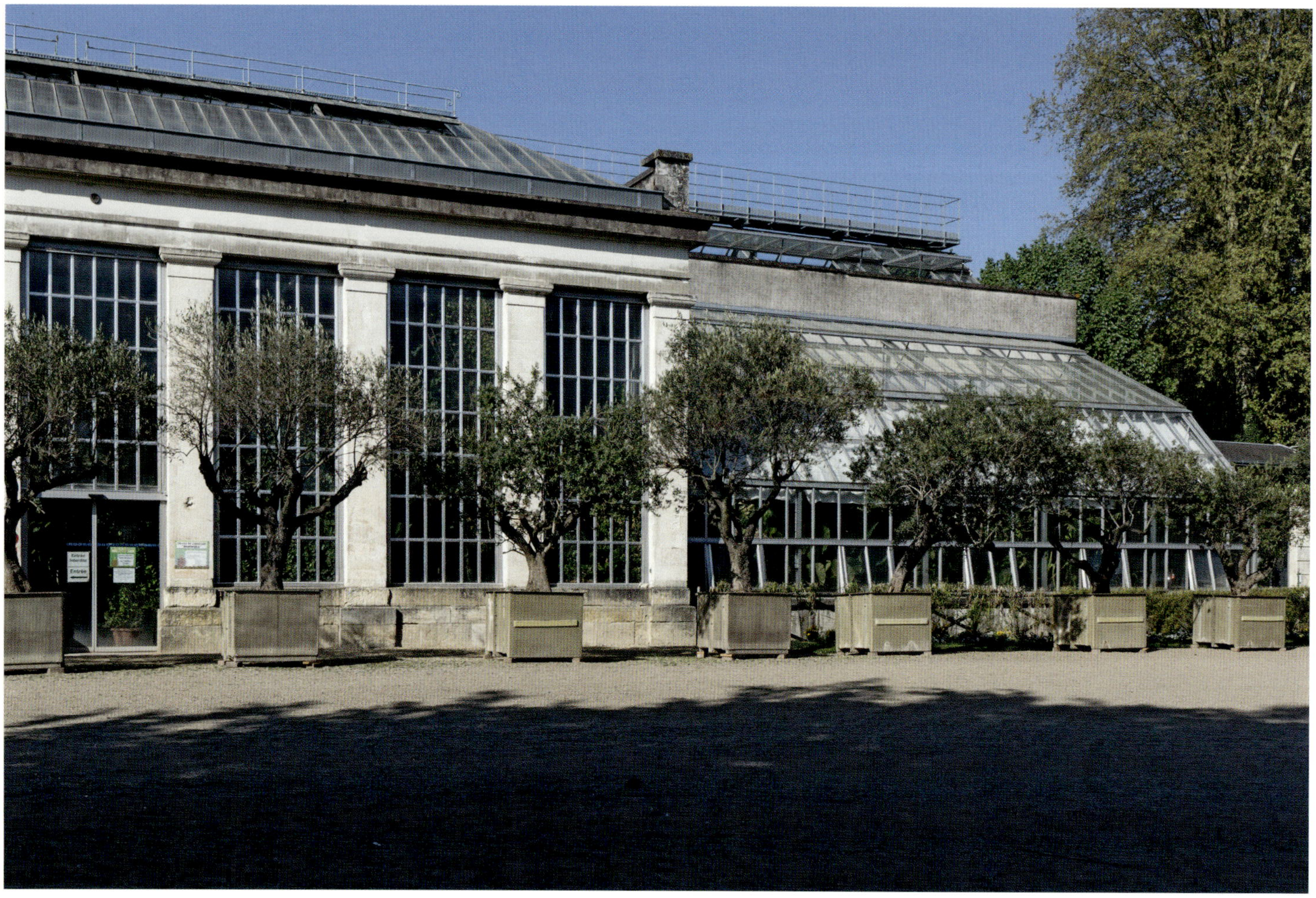

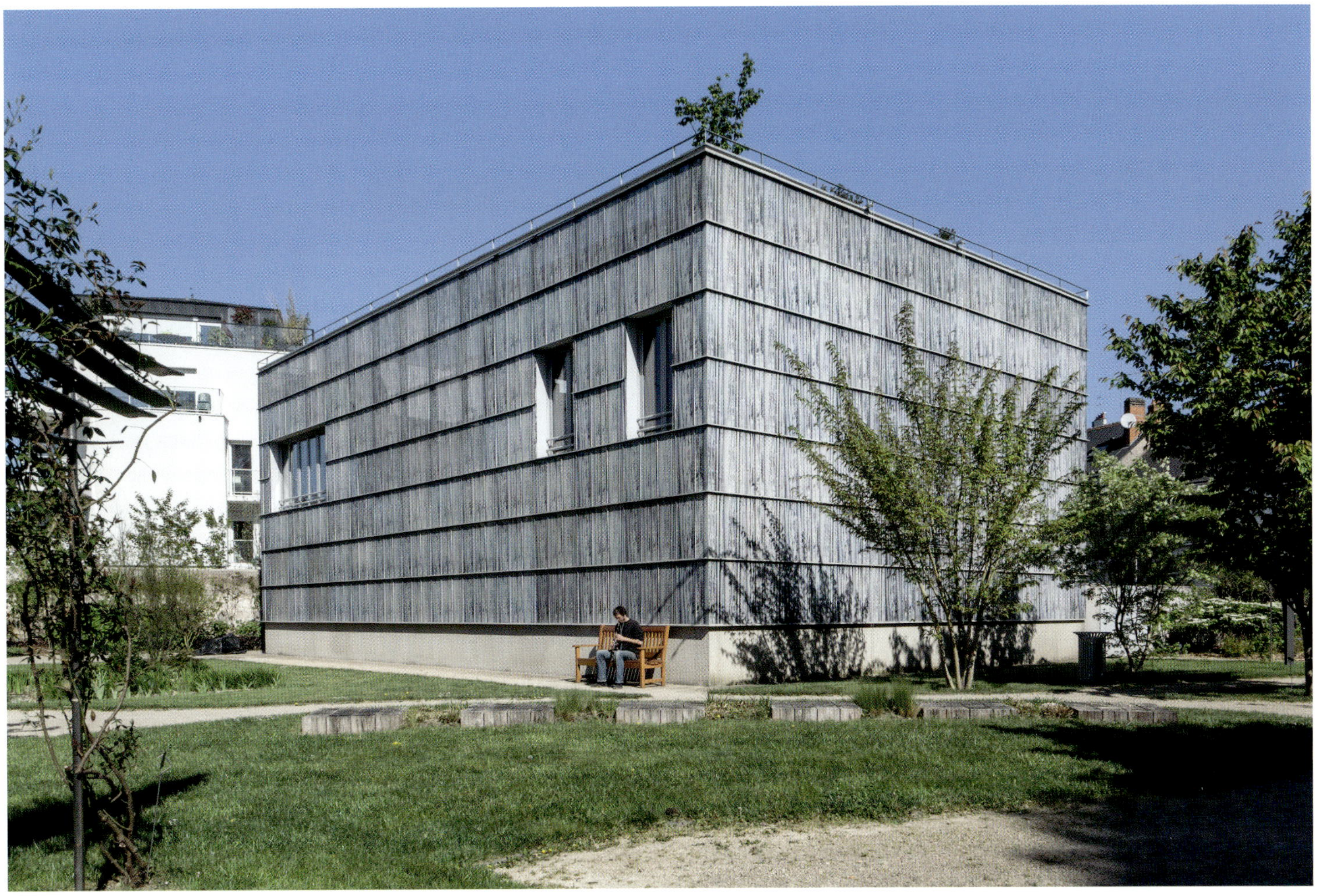

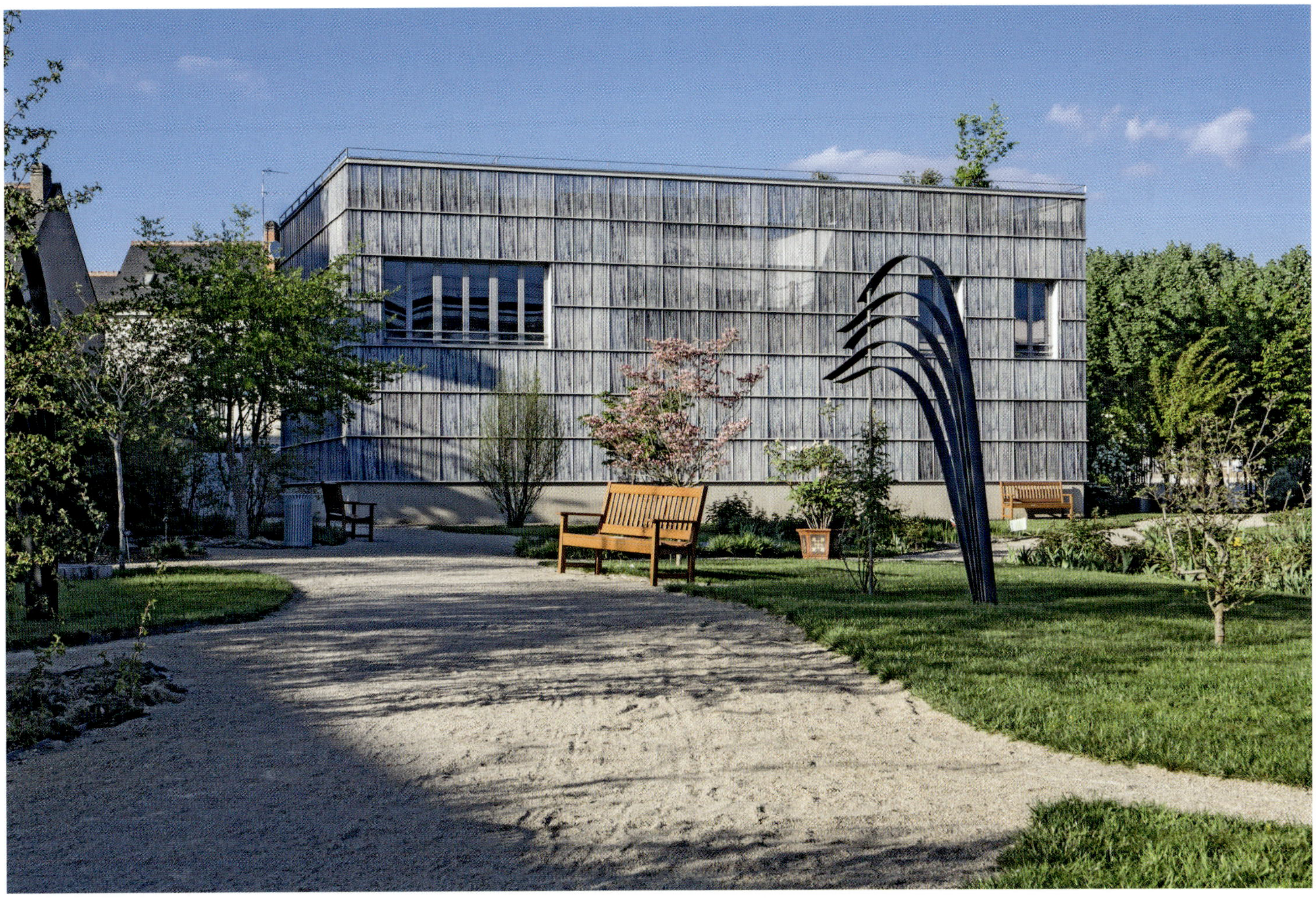

8. Detailed view of the greenhouse façade.
9. Side view of the greenhouse.
10. Interior of the restored old greenhouse.

Covered tennis courts in Vanves, Hauts-de-Seine, 2003–06

At the Parc André Roche in Vanves (Hauts-de-Seine), a protected natural site, the construction of two covered tennis courts was planned as part of the enlargement of an existing sports area in a municipality lacking in such facilities. The 1,458 m² programme set a double challenge: on the one hand it required tall volumes with specific light and acoustic qualities, and on the other it necessitated an architecture that would blend well into its natural surroundings.

In response to these constraints, Barrier chose the most resistant and functional structure imaginable: five arches in glulam constitute the loadbearing structure of each court, their dimensions calculated according to the parameters of the game they must contain. With a minimum of material, they sketch out a succession of lines that clearly circumscribe the building volume, while metal cross-bracing allows fixing of the curved polycarbonate cladding panels which, thanks to their green-tinted translucency, let in maximum natural light. A second metal structure, in the form of a horizontal grill, carries artificial lighting. Again, with a minimum of material, the metal harmonizes with the wooden structure, since together they sketch out a graphic play of fine lines in space. At once functional and aesthetic, the ensemble distantly recalls one of the Perret brothers' first buildings, the celebrated 1903 Esders workshop in Paris.

Combinations of wood and metal are a recurrent avenue of exploration in Barrier's work, always guided by a concern to use each material according to its intrinsic structural properties and to ensure the readability of each part in the whole. The open, translucent roof volume sits above a more compact block, clad inside with wood, which, through its texture and warm hue, links the ensemble visually to the clay court. Thanks to a horizontal brise-soleil set over the building, sunlight is filtered to reduce glare, while luminosity is further augmented by a glazed lateral façade that also offers the sensation of being both outside and in at the same time.

On the exterior, the roof, with its effect of dematerialization, is balanced by the solid of the volume below, whose façades, located on the lower part of the sloping terrain, sit on a dark-metal base. They are clad in five bands of aluminium onto which a vegetal motif has been printed, creating a continuous line linking the building to the neighbouring structures. These horizontal sequences lead the eye to the level of the park and help integrate the building, despite its very particular massing, into its surroundings. The remarkable foliage motif both recalls and updates late-19th-century vegetal patterns as used in ironwork, furniture or kiosks in public parks and gardens.

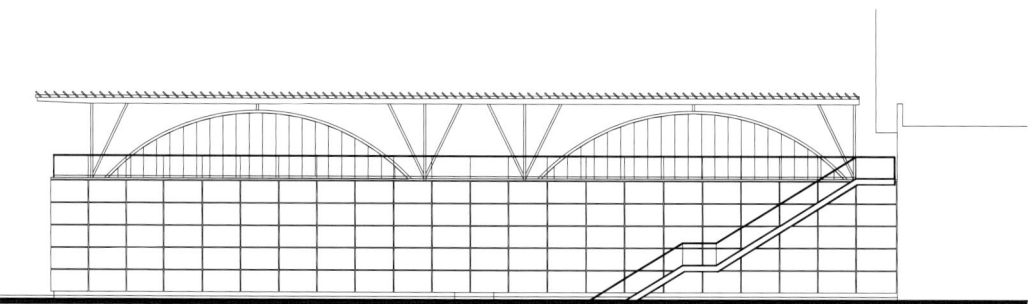

FACADE

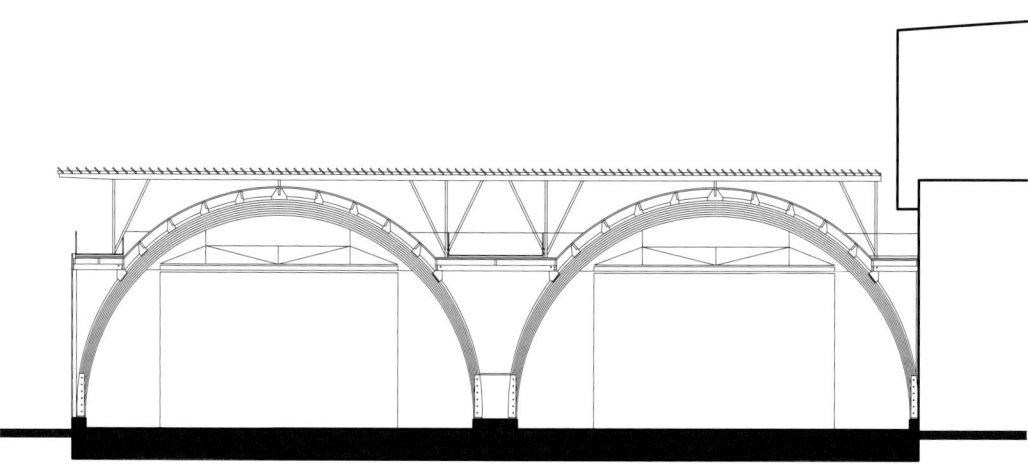

COUPE

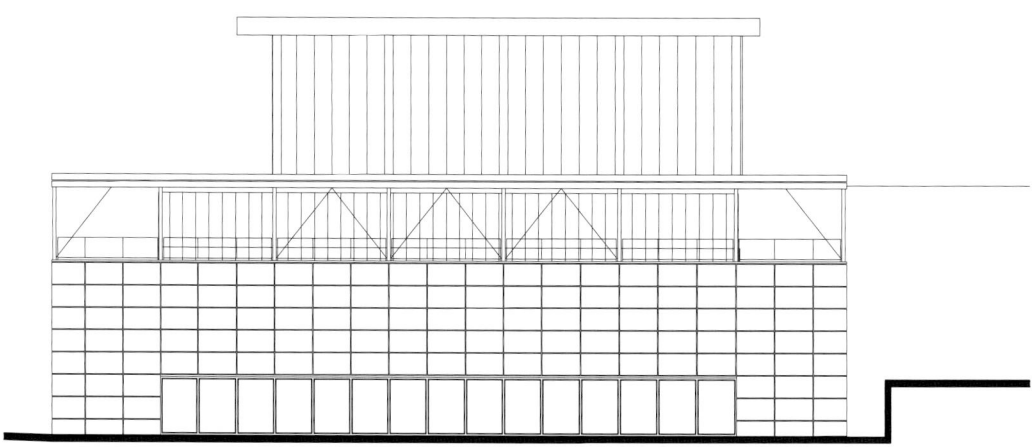

FACADE

1. Elevations and section.
2. Front facing the park.

3, 4. Interior views.

Cap 55, Saint-Pierre-des-Corps, Indre-et-Loire, 2009–21

In mid-1970s, after its post-war reconstruction on a linear plan running parallel to the station and the train tracks, Saint-Pierre-des-Corps began to pursue a rather different urban vision, which included the decision to allocate more than half of its territory to business activities. The arrival of the TGV in 1990 made the neighbourhood around the station particularly attractive, and to this day it still benefits from the available building plots near this important transport hub.

Construction of the TGV station also prompted Saint-Pierre-des-Corps's planning department to rethink the future of the town centre and the neighbouring areas. In the context of decisions taken in the late 1980s, Barrier had already built the municipal library, the Line-Porcher School and the cultural centre, as well as designing the reconfiguration of the Avenue Jean-Bonnin, planned for the arrival of a tram line that has yet to materialize. Where the area near the railway was concerned, Barrier, who also designed the square in front of the TGV station, was initially asked to come up with ideas for the wider zone, the goal being to create a continuity between the station, its square and its platforms to facilitate connection with the town centre. But this new urban composition later had to take into account another request from the planning department: the creation of a sight line from the train tracks towards Tours Cathedral, a diagonal perspective that would henceforth regulate the layout of the entire neighbourhood.

The Cap 55 office complex is located between the Rue Fabienne-Landy and this new axis, on a wedge-shaped site. Programmed in three phases, the ensemble will comprise 12,000 m² of high-energy-performance office space to be fitted out by the occupants. In plan, the complex articulates two main buildings in the shape of an inversed L, thereby marking out the new street layout in three dimensions as well as forming a planted courtyard that will provide a new pedestrian access to the town centre. The third building, closing the site at its prow, is the stand-out element in the composition, and will mark the entrance to the station quarter. Together, the three structures reconfigure the urban block and create a new space that is directly accessible to train passengers.

The smooth, carefully detailed building envelope alternates black and white, a nod to railway signals, with an inversion of black building/white perforated screen, white building/black perforated screen. The three wings are united by a dark base in slab-marked concrete, which anchors them visually to the ground. The random play of larger glazing ensembles expresses the presence of meeting rooms, while the double skin in folded perforated steel covering the western and southern façades (which have regular fenestration) acts as both a brise-soleil and insulation to regulate inside temperature. In this way, the façade becomes a true »light machine«.

1. Site plan.
2, 3. Plan and elevation.
4. Façades overlooking the interior space.

pp. 36, 37
5. Entrance from Rue Fabienne-Landy.
6. The large interior patio.

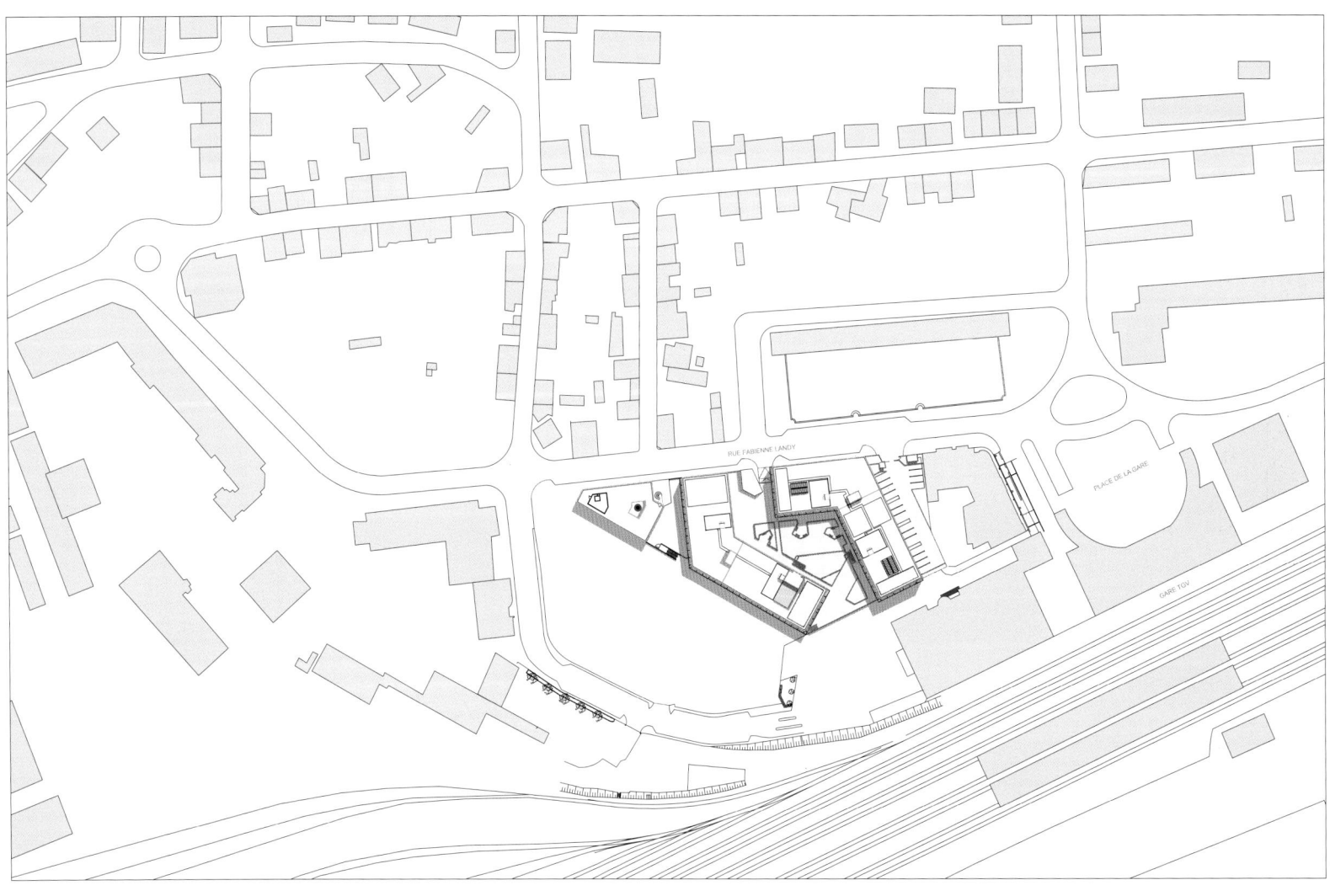

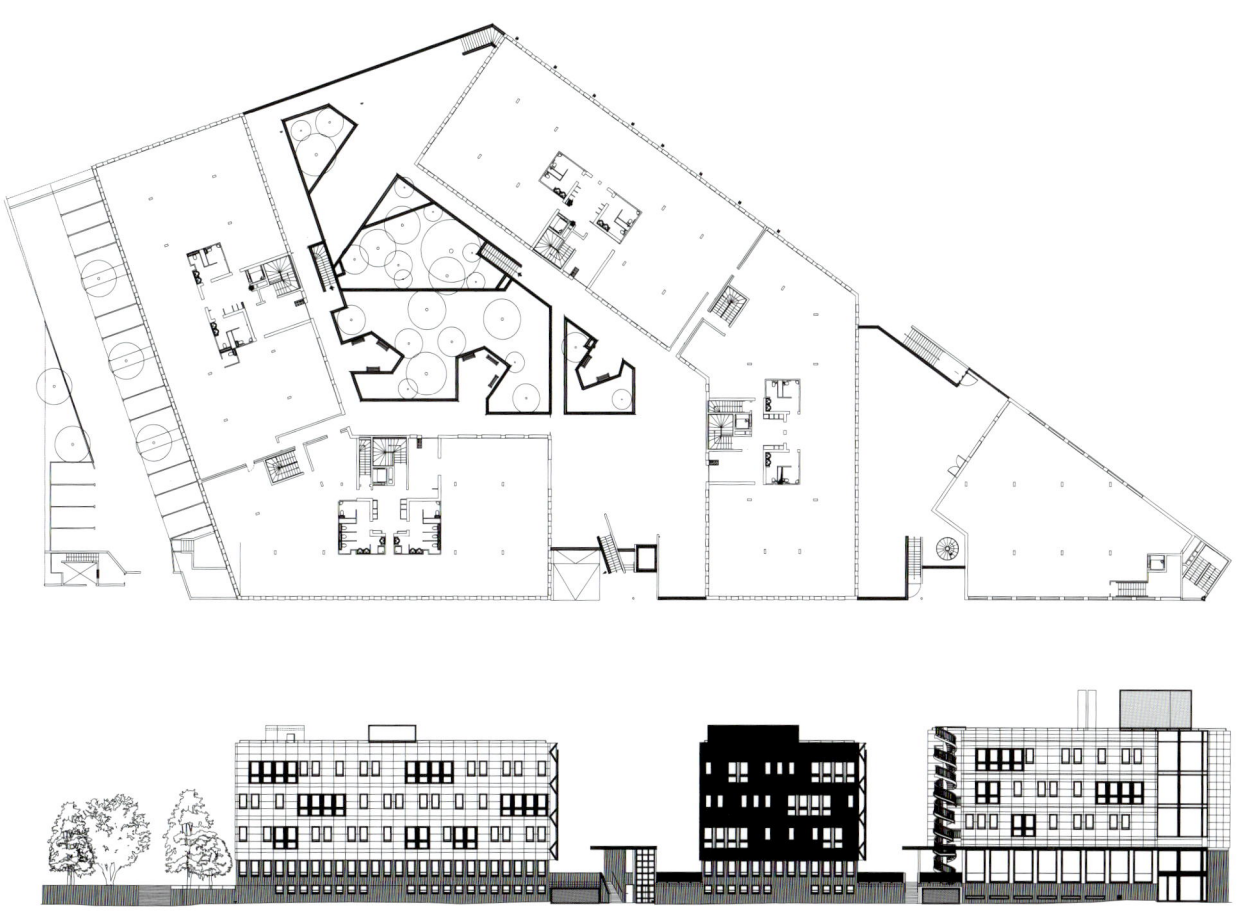

7, 8. Detailed view of the sun-protected façades.

Urban elevator in Chinon, Indre-et-Loire, 2006–08

This elevator, which links the lower and upper town, is the first phase in a reconfiguration of the historic centre of Chinon. In its final version, the programme was to include an infant school, housing and accommodation for the municipality, the goal being to recreate the scale and density of the original neighbourhood, which was destroyed by a landslide in the early 20th century. To date, only the elevator has been built.

Completed in 2008, this urban lift links the shops and services in the dense medieval streets of the lower town to upper Chinon, which is dominated by the celebrated castle – dating back to the 10th century, it attracts over 100,000 visitors a year – but is also home to housing and shopping centres. Both client and architect agreed that the main objective was to build a highly technical piece of engineering infrastructure that, though a new addition to the historic fabric of Chinon, would blend in with it using a contemporary vocabulary and would connect the different strata of the town's architectural morphology.

The elevator integrates very naturally into its context by extending the streets leading up towards the hillside. Backing onto a rocky outcrop, it locks into the historic pathways leading from the Vienne to the hill, as though it were simply their »mechanized« continuation. At its summit, a 13 m-long timber-and-steel footbridge links the lift to the hillside, and is oriented diagonally, in a gesture of politeness, towards the castle. The natural pedestrian flow thus continues towards the fortress, and vice versa when coming down from the summit towards the lower town.

With its two 16-person cabins contained in an elegant, soaring 27 m-high tower, the elevator forms a contemporary urban signal that revitalizes and ennobles a hitherto neglected neighbourhood. Through its architectural approach, the lift engages in a complex dialogue with the surrounding urbanity. Its lower part is in raw concrete, thereby echoing the ashlar of the houses built into the hillside. The upper part, on the other hand, is far more dematerialized thanks to its structure in steel, whose blue tint echoes Chinon's slate roofs, an effect that is reinforced by the elevator's own roof, which takes the form of a flattened diamond, thereby evoking historic forms. The first part of the journey up is blind, but as you reach the top you enjoy a panoramic view over the entire valley, thereby transposing almost metaphorically the »ascension« into an architectural form. At the same time, the upper part's transparency takes away all monumentality from this »vertical link« and allows it almost to »disappear« in the townscape.

The search for harmony and dialogue with the surroundings also drives the relationship between the different parts that go to make up this piece of engineering – a balance between solid and void coupled with harmonious proportions established from a basic module that is repeated in every detail, as well as a graphic silhouette that ensures continuity between the concrete base and the steel summit. One of the few examples of its type in Europe, this new urban elevator erases a natural frontier that is literally as old as the hills.

1. Access from the town centre.
2. Cross-section showing the site integration.
3. Access from the road to the château.

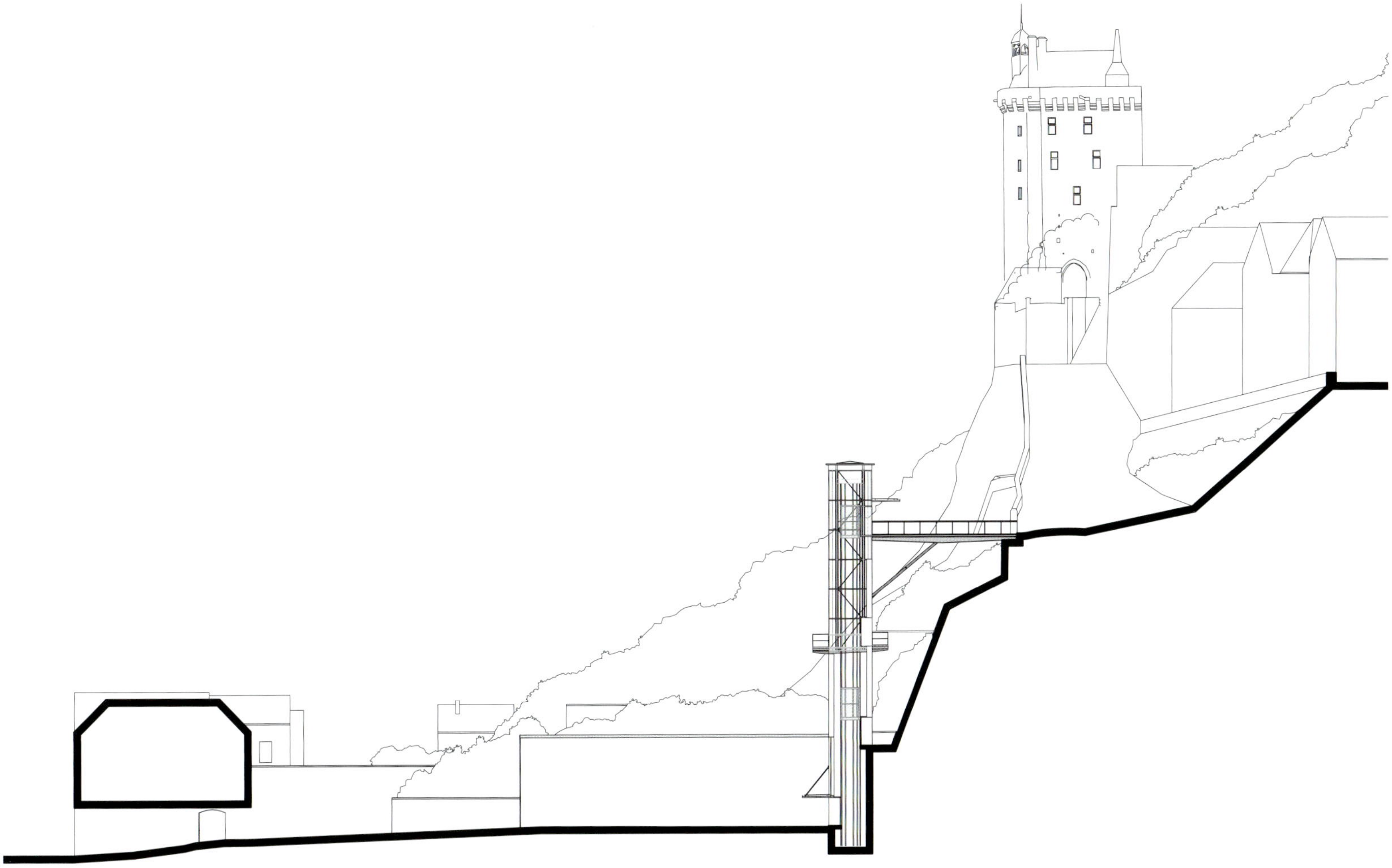

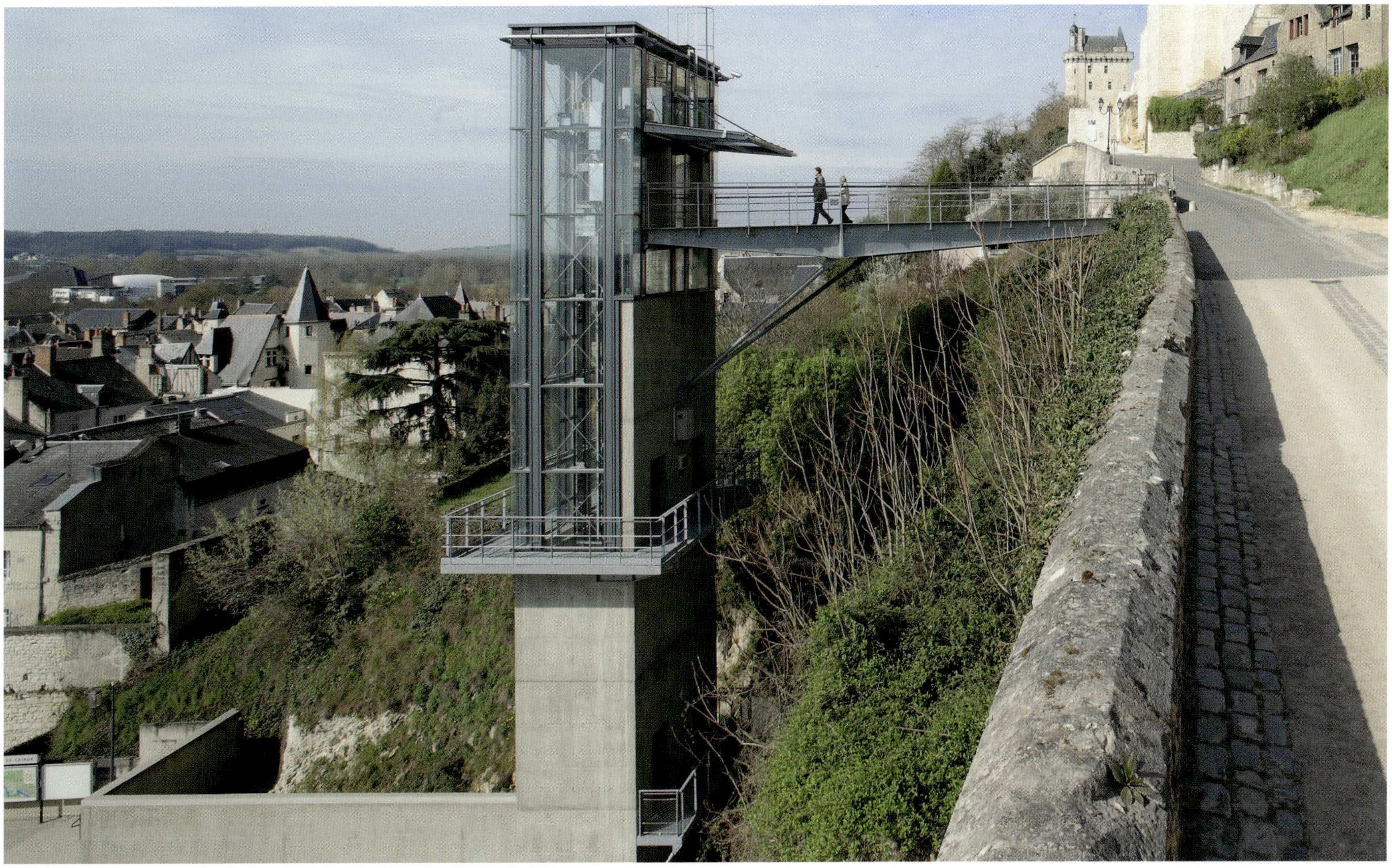

Les Papeteries de Bretagne redevelopment, Rennes, Ille-et-Vilaine, 2006–13

After the Papeteries de Bretagne paper factory closed, in 1999, its 17,000 m² site on the river Vilaine near central Rennes came up for redevelopment. The city added an adjoining 20,000 m² and set about planning a new neighbourhood of housing and offices. Located in the Moulin du Comte sector, which was undergoing rehabilitation, the Papeteries de Bretagne redevelopment was aligned with the overall objectives of this operation. An exceptional undertaking, enjoying 240 m of south-facing façades along the Vilaine, the redevelopment comprises 5,000 m² of offices, 68 social-housing units, 87 dwellings for senior citizens and 119 affordable properties for purchase, of which 11 are town houses.

On the river front, four identical ten-storey south-facing blocks stand side by side; behind them, another four identical seven-storey blocks rise in a staggered sequence. Three other structures mark the edges of the site: to the west, the 11 terraced houses, which ensure a link to the existing urban fabric; to the east, a six-storey office building with a comb-shaped plan; and to the north, two further buildings placed horizontally in front of the four seven-storey blocks. A network of streets and pathways, articulated by small squares and fountains, comprises the new neighbourhood's infrastructure.

Due to the risk of flooding, the river-front blocks are raised up on bases containing parking, so that their entrance floors and internal access routes sit well above the high-water level. Moreover, the car park's waterproof wall forms a dyke that protects the rest of the site, while hydraulic discharge reservoirs compensate for the expansion volume of the river before urbanization.

The density of housing, offices and infrastructure forms a true urban landscape, which is modelled through the relationship of the buildings to each other, in particular the height gradation with respect to the river. The various programmes are organized so as to create an urban and functional mix that provides multiple forms of dwelling on a single site. Routes through the development also evoke the idea of a city with its visual markers and network of different types of thoroughfare: streets, pedestrian alleys, suspended walkways, covered arcades, pavements and stairs ensure access to the reconstituted tow path as well as allowing views out towards the river, while the inclusion of small squares accentuates the urban character. An intriguing ball-like sculpture on a pedestal stands at the centre of the main square: it is in fact the pulp mixer, a vestige of the old paper factory that evokes the memory of place while providing an urban landmark and structuring the spatial organization.

While the first founding principle of the redevelopment is the creation of an urban landscape, the second is water. To this end, the staggered siting of the buildings allows every dwelling to enjoy uninterrupted southern views over the gardens, the reservoirs and the river, while the upper floors command stunning panoramas across the whole of Rennes. The relationship with water is also found in the way the mass and monumentality of the housing blocks and office buildings is dissolved: the composition of the façades, with their different projecting volumes, balconies and awnings, lightens the volume of these urban villas with an elegance that is also to be found in the use of polycarbonate, a light, translucent and opaque material. The riverside elevations, perched up on pilotis, also enjoy finely wrought balconies and projecting volumes that diminish in bulk as they rise. Their reflection in the water accentuates this dematerialization and becomes the principal theme for the formal organization of all the buildings on the Papeteries de Bretagne site.

1. Site plan.
2. General view across the Vilaine River.
3. Side façade across a water basin.

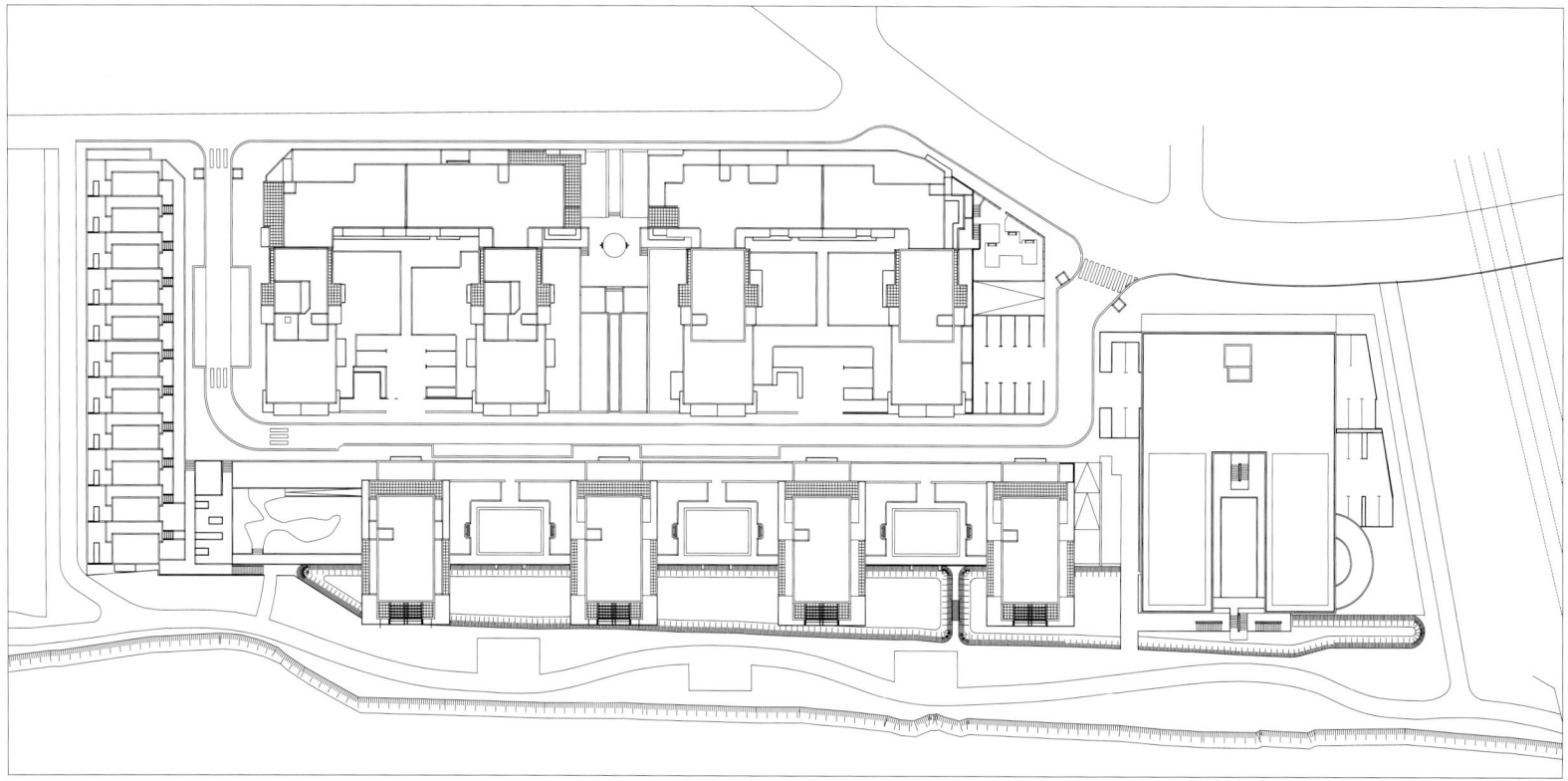

4. *La Lessiveuse*, memory of the old paper mill.
5, 6. The houses in a row.

Résidence Carré Verde, Vertou, Loire-Atlantique, 2009–13

Launched following the partial demolition of a hospital, the Carré Verde operation is an urban redevelopment scheme in the centre of Vertou, to the south of Nantes. By extending the centre towards the Place du Beau-Berger and articulating old and new around the Place Saint-Martin, the municipality sought to welcome not only new inhabitants but also shops and services in an urban form that would bring renewed intensity to the historic heart. Begun in the summer of 2009 and completed in April 2013, the redevelopment comprises four main urban parcels containing 109 dwellings (30 % social sector) and 10,000 m² of retail and service space, as well as all the public areas – streets, squares, gardens, and pathways – that go to make up a new neighbourhood.

Of the original fabric, only one 19th-century building had been kept (converted into a library), while a new music school had been built. Given the demolitions, there was very little architectural or urban context to work with – besides the school and the library, the only spatial and architectural landmarks were the church, the municipal cemetery and a rather loose scattering of suburban shops and houses. Right from the start, the project was guided by the idea of creating a coherent and structured parcel of urbanity with all the usual links and continuities in relation to the immediate environment, as well as a new point of convergence and centrality in the form of a large paved area by the Place du Beau-Verger. The underlying objective was to create an »urban architecture« in which the urban and architectonic forms would create a coherent spatial and conceptual entity.

The siting of the various buildings picks up on the existing street pattern so as to create new urban blocks that reinforce and accentuate the historic configuration. Rising three or four stories, and crowned with an attic floor, the buildings follow the street line, thereby ensuring lively fronts along the Rue Bonnigal and the Place du Beau-Verger, which are cadenced by the columns of the retail units and entrance halls. In the pedestrian streets, the buildings are more discreet, taking the form of small, domestic-scale town houses that allow glimpses into the gardens behind. Where the land rises, a large pedestrian space in the form of a stairway provides an almost theatrical view onto the surrounding landscape, while north–south and east–west cross routes allow the scale of the development to be adjusted to the immediate surroundings. Opposite the monumental verticality of the church, the new structures ensure a suitable identity for the neighbourhood.

The architectural approach takes its cue from the spirit of generosity that defined the urban planning. Rather than compact volumes, the four buildings are formally diverse, evoking the idea of apartment blocks and town houses. With their double envelope, their play of projecting and retreating volumes and their soigné detailing (brise-soleils, generous balconies, shutters, stairways, lifts and the use of colour), the buildings fit into the free spirit of the redevelopment while renewing the architectural and urban quality of central Vertou. This concern for quality is also to be found in the treatment of communal spaces and appointments: besides being sources of daylight and transitional zones between outside and in, the balconies and terraces provide »extra« living space, while the handling of the façades ensures that each dwelling enjoys its own distinct identity.

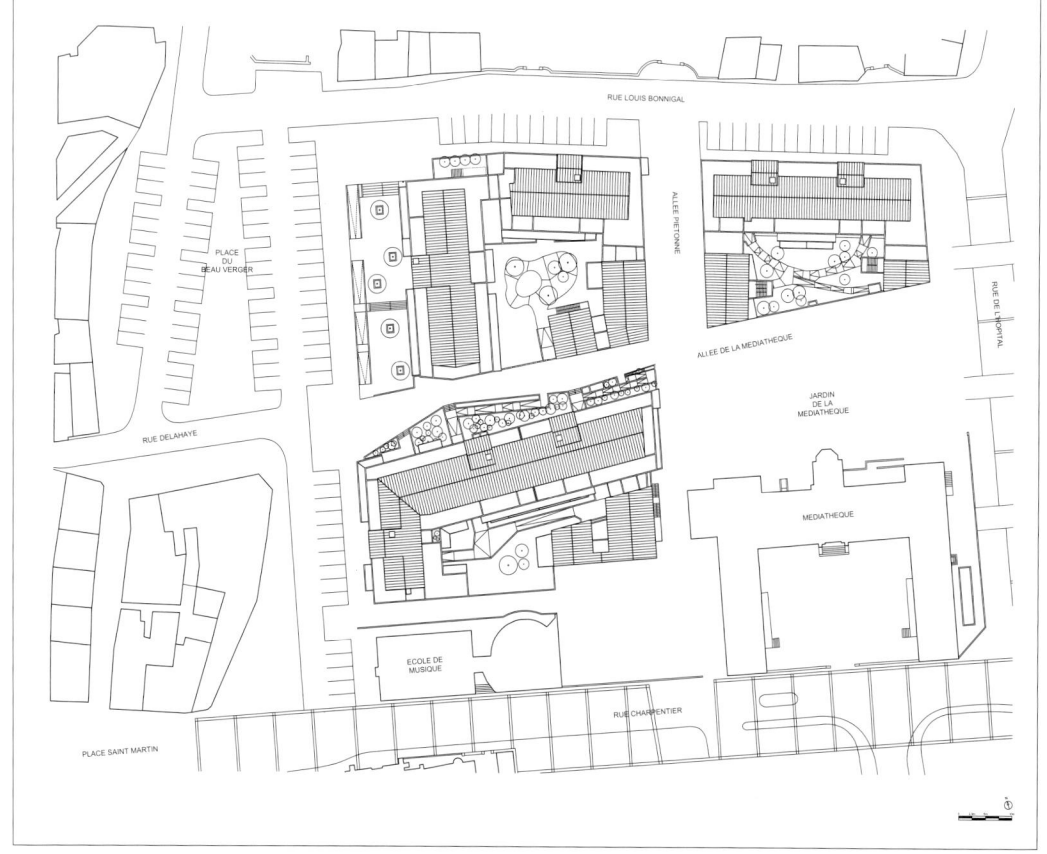

1. Site plan.
2. West façade overlooking the public space.
3. View towards the church.

pp. 48, 49
4, 5. The inner street with the accompanying houses.
6. The stepped central space.

Résidence Les Brandons, Blainville-sur-Orne, Calvados, 2000–07

In 1920, the Société d'habitation à bon marché de Blainville-sur-Orne built a new neighbourhood, Les Brandons, for workers at the shipyards near Caen: located on the left bank of the canal, and organized in groups of four, the 110 houses all enjoyed enormous 500 m² gardens so that the occupants could grow their own produce. By the end of the 20th century, however, Les Brandons had fallen into a sorry state: the built fabric was deteriorating, the gardens were too big to be maintained and over half the dwellings were empty. An ageing population occupied the remainder, nostalgic for times gone by.

In 1988, because of the neighbourhood's handy location near the centre of Blainville-sur-Orne, the municipality and La Plaine Normandie (the social-housing company that owned the site) set about redeveloping it. The old houses, which were difficult to bring up to modern standards, were to be demolished and replaced by a contemporary architectural ensemble that would include a strong landscape component in its design. To ensure smooth rehousing of the remaining inhabitants, the operation was programmed in successive phases.

Barrier maintained the existing street structure and topographic features of Les Brandons, designing a contemporary garden-city in the spirit of its predecessor but with greater typological variety: small apartment buildings and urban villas set in parkland, and town houses with patios and gardens, form an ensemble of renewed urban diversity. The four plots are all divided up in the same way: the street line is expressed by the apartment buildings at either end and framed by the town houses, while urban courtyards allow privacy within the block. The plots in the middle, in the form of strips, create depth through a carefully controlled sequence of dwelling, garden-patio, semi-public square, garage. Pulled slightly back from the building line, the houses are protected by planting.

In order to increase the offer of both rental and freehold properties and welcome a new, younger population, the operation sought significant densification, with 240 dwellings instead of the original 70. The new street plan, more urban in form, facilitates this goal. Small front gardens, entrance gates, abundant vegetation and careful design of public spaces ensure both conviviality and individual appropriation. Even if there is a strong social-sector aspect to the development, the architectural approach seeks, through both its urban composition and its vocabulary, to reinvent collective living. Repetition has been avoided, and each type of dwelling has its own distinct form, so that every home is personalized – an individualization that is reinforced by the use of colour. Materials are also mixed: masonry, wood and metal, always carefully detailed, with timber cladding for the garages, annexes and upper floors, resulting in a warm, welcoming ensemble. Spacious and flooded with sunshine, the apartments are often double aspect front–back, while pergolas and long balconies create a play of light and shade. The care taken with respect to the social aspect and quality of life recalls one of the first German eco-neighbourhoods, the 1993–2006 Vauban development in Freiburg im Breisgau.

1. Site plan.
2. Access road between the rows of houses.

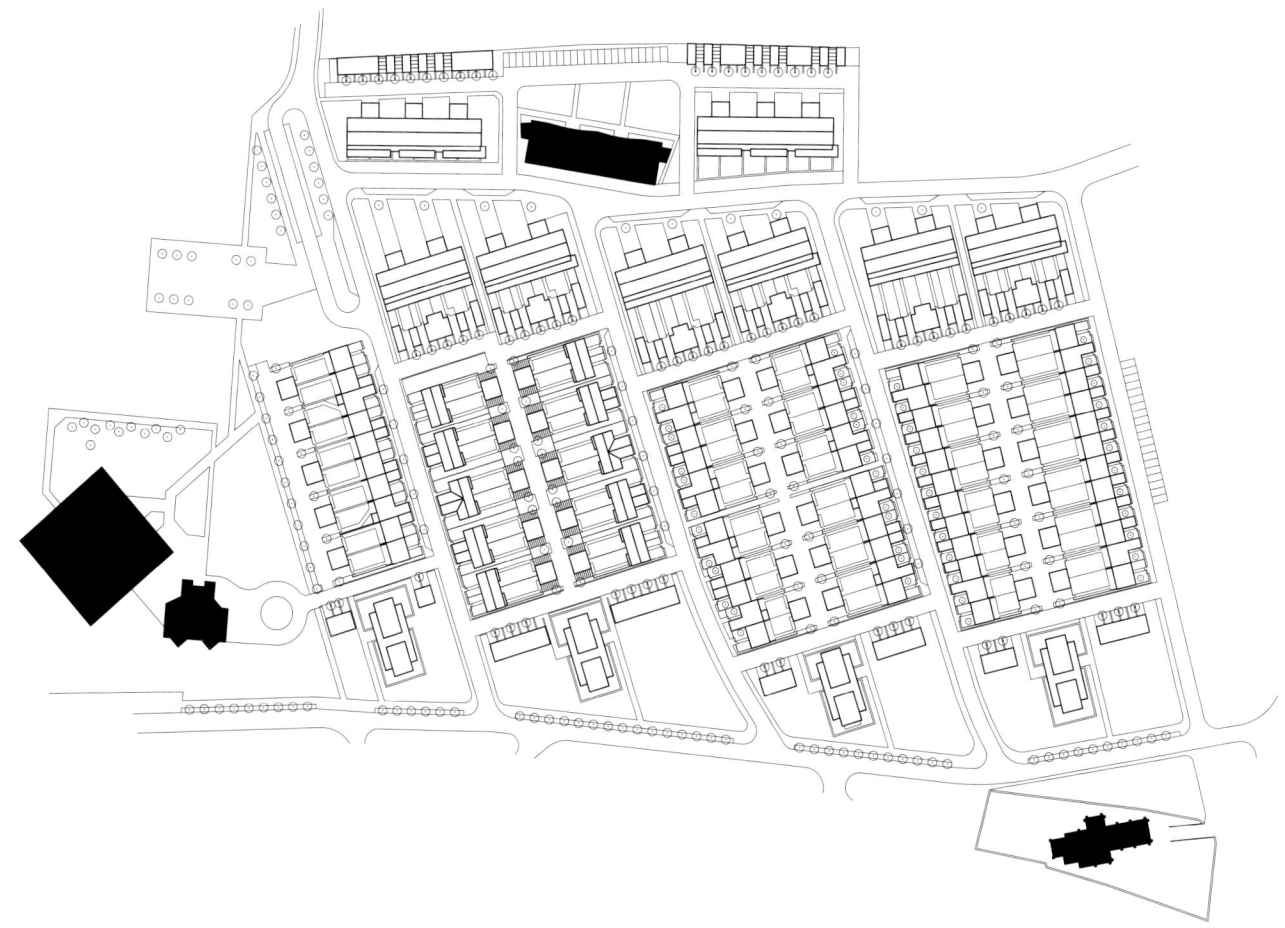

3. One of the apartment buildings.
4. The urban atmosphere of the new neighbourhood.

La Guignardière eco-neighbourhood, Chambray-lès-Tours, Indre-et-Loire, 2016–23

Launched by the town council of Chambray-lès-Tours at a public meeting in December 2015, the La Guignardière eco-neighbourhood was initially to have been built by a developer, but in the end the municipality decided to undertake the operation itself, commissioning Barrier as advising architect. Work began in 2016 and is expected to complete in 2026.

The philosophy of La Guignardière builds on the heritage of the first European eco-neighbourhoods, of which the Vauban development in the German town of Freiburg im Breisgau (1993–2006) remains a model of sustainable urban planning. To reduce its ecological impact, La Guignardière takes into account every environmental factor, setting ambitious targets for each. Among them are energy sobriety and transport, with a reduction in use of the motor car and encouragement of soft transportation. Attention must also be paid to the choice of materials and the construction process: bio-sourcing, reduction and recycling of waste, reduction in the quantity of water used, and preservation of bio-diversity. But in addition to measures to reduce the impact of construction on the environment, the project englobes a much wider vision with respect to sustainable design: the management of water and of air quality, as well as the use of colour (white roofing for example) to reduce heat gain. All of this is second nature to Barrier, who has long been concerned by environmental and ecological considerations – he built one of the first solar houses in France, as well as bioclimatic, biotic, and timber-framed homes, and, in 2001, completed the rammed-earth Salvatierra apartment building in Rennes, part of the European Cepheus programme. Today these projects are considered pioneers of eco-design.

In total, La Guignardière will provide 55,000 m² of housing: 600 dwellings, of which 25 % will be social sector (with a mix of generations and income levels), 30 % for sale at affordable rates and 45 % at market price. Typologies will also be mixed, with 40 % of collective and intermediary dwellings and 60 % of individual houses. In addition, a 1,300 m² parcel will be allocated to construction of a 270 m² neighbourhood centre (by Atelier RVL Architectes), 1,200 m² of mostly ground-floor accommodation will be allocated to business activities, and there will be 1,500 m² of public squares, 8,000 m² of allotments (equipped with garden sheds, fences and rainwater collectors) and a 4,350 m² park, to be landscaped by the winners of a national design competition.

These figures show that there is a strong focus on bio–diversity with 50 % green spaces (urban park, shared gardens, squares and playgrounds) and the creation of a vegetation network that includes (excluding the Bois de la Guignardière) nearly 25 % of the district, not counting all the private spaces: gardens, hedges, planted fringes, urban courtyards, green roofs, tree-lined squares, etc.

While the environmental approach is primordial, La Guignardière's particularity is also to be found in its urban plan, which is based on an organic approach that structures access, entries, links with the neighbouring environment, public spaces (the main square, smaller squares, the park, the valley, ponds and reservoirs, the allotments) as well as the varied network of soft-transport pathways (horse, bike and pedestrian), principal vehicle thoroughfares, secondary thoroughfares, urban courtyards and parking. The main southern path, which arrives in the heart of the neighbourhood in the axis of the main square and the neighbourhood centre, will be laid out as a pedestrian/bike route running alongside a canal that will collect rainwater from the hamlets to be built on either side.

The method used to make sure these choices are respected is the guidance plan, a reference document that represents the neighbourhood in its finished state while leaving room for dialogue. An evolving tool, it will define the urban character of the development according to a number of themes, including: village living, the occupation of gardens, workshops, terraces, rooftops, squares, streets, urban villas and houses with patios. Other themes will reinforce social cohesion and contribute to the creation of a lively neighbourhood: business activities in the main square, the presence of a crèche and the neighbourhood centre, in addition to the generous public spaces (the park, the squares, the wood, the allotments, themed and creative gardens). For each plot there is a description of the expected urban and architectural ambiances, with guidelines setting out the goals for the different programmes. Every individual project must follow the guidance plan and its planning recommendations in order to achieve a coherent global result.

Another particularity of La Guignardière is the search for an architectural quality specific to the ensemble, one that will not simply be expressed by an overall coherence between the small and intermediary apartment buildings and the groups of town ,houses but also by the integration of small hamlets of individual houses with gardens. This is why the development also includes an area of architect-designed houses, in order to satisfy a strong demand for empty plots: in the third phase, around 30 parcels of around 400 m² each will be made available, an original approach undertaken in partnership with the Maison de l'Architecture Centre-Val de Loire to establish a catalogue of young French architecture offices that have already built houses with the quality, sensibility and/or sense of innovation required for the prescriptions of an eco-neighbourhood. Future buyers will be able to choose their home according to their affinities from the list proposed in the catalogue.

Architectural offices working at La Guignardière include AUA Paul Chemetov, Mill Architecture, RVL, Ivars et Ballet, Bertrand Penneron and MU, with Geoplus for the urban infrastructure.

1. Site plan.

Résidence Le Bois, Moult, Calvados, 2010/11

Located near the centre of Moult, in a recently constructed suburban development offering no contextual cues, the Le Bois housing estate seeks, through its spatiality, a new form of planning that will also clarify the relationship to the existing built fabric. The 44 detached social-sector houses, offering between two and five bedrooms (75 to 110 m²), occupy a site on the edge of a disused quarry that has been converted into a park.

What might have become a simple surveyor's division, with uniform cookie-cutter plots, is instead a true urban composition with a complex structure of public and private space organized according to an equilibrium between solid and void, built and unbuilt, open and closed. Unexpected views and perspectives, and the alternating types of space avoid the repetitive aspect that might have resulted from the serial nature of a development made up of cubic volumes.

The result is a small neighbourhood grouped around a central esplanade that is lined on two sides by party-wall houses in groups of two and four. This large rectangle, which is crossed by a planted pedestrian pathway, is partly surrounded by a second row of detached houses and another series of party-wall dwellings that are deliberately not lined up with the rest. In this way, an organic plan is created, while smaller built volumes – garages, garden sheds, projections – balance and structure yet further the ensemble.

A diversity of typologies in a controlled spatial layout makes this operation a true piece of »urban surgery« that restructures the neighbouring suburban development. The subtlety of the plan, in its balance and gradation, is picked up in the architectural approach through the progressive transition from private house to public space: each dwelling features a fluid relationship between outside and in thanks to the spatial sequences between the garages, second parking spaces, storage areas, houses, terraces, private patios, gardens, pathways, pergolas, etc. All these spaces, whether built, empty or landscaped, form an organic ensemble.

Even if every house takes on the same simple cubic form, they are individualized thanks to unusual architectural features: huge patio-like covered porches, many of them double height, provide shelter as you arrive, magnifying and dramatizing the entrance while providing extra living space. The façades display a chromatic palette that, nuancing blacks and whites, progressively transitions to grey-green pastel shades in a contemporary reinterpretation of the hues of typical half-timbered houses in the Pays d'Auge, a nod to local architectural traditions. This use of colour in a very graphic manner also helps to disguise the fact that all the houses are built to the same plan with the same materials and the same timber frame. Thanks to this architectural trick, an identical materiality changes its physical, tactile and aesthetic aspect, the colouring of the wood becoming denser the closer you get to the heart of the development. The 90 cm-long façade shingles are hung horizontally to create an abstract design which provides a visual rhythm that balances out the different built volumes, a graphic quality that is further enhanced by the form and disposition (sometimes asymmetrical) of the fenestration.

A small, two-class school completes the estate, realized with the same formal simplicity and wooden cladding as the housing. As with other Barrier projects of this type, Le Blois demonstrates that an architectural approach can overcome the usual monotony of social housing all the while ensuring a better use of space and a more pleasant living environment.

1. Site plan.
2. Street façades.
3. Private space with garden sheds.

4. The large interior square.
5. The paths under the pergolas.
6. Private entrances under porches.

Résidence Blériot, Tours, Indre-et-Loire, 2011–15

Located on the site of the Vieux Colombier – a former farm once belonging to the Abbaye de Marmoutier, of which a few vestiges survive – opposite the Monconseil development area, the Blériot housing block is located to the north of Tours, where most of the city's recent expansion has occurred, away from flood zones.

The initial masterplan consisted of three identical L-plan buildings but, after testing the idea, Barrier found it unconvincing and instead proposed a single H plan set perpendicular to the street on a north–south through axis: two wings frame a large, translucent, glass-clad structure containing stairs, lifts, access landings and a winter garden, a solution he had already tried out at Mordelles, near Rennes, with his 2005 Les Glénans operation. The greenhouse-type structure, which links two wings each containing ten dwellings, constitutes a transitional space with respect to thermal issues, as well as a shared, protected area that allows sheltered access in bad weather and plantings by the residents.

The idea of linking different wings by a covered internal courtyard recalls the Familistère de Guise (Aisne), which was designed and built between 1859 and 1883 by the industrialist Jean-Baptiste Godin. In this new »social palace«, the natural light brought down into the interior encouraged communication between the residents in collective spaces of conviviality, exchange and sharing. Such meeting spaces are also to be found in organic modernism and in 1950s European archi-

tectural experiments, such as Finnish architect Alvar Aalto's 1957 INTERBAU (Internationale Bauausstellung/International Building Exhibition) housing project in Berlin, where the dwellings are »prolonged« by shared spaces of exchange such as large landings and generous, light-filled corridors.

Besides the creation of the sunny interior »greenhouse«, the design of the Blériot apartments themselves aims to bring in a maximum of daylight, their through accommodation, which is prolonged by a generous balcony that acts as an extra room, being constantly filled with natural illumination. Indeed, the theme of light is the leitmotiv of the whole development, the choice of materials and their deployment being another way of conceptualizing the idea. The translucent and opaque aspect of the planar envelope in crystal Danpalon BRV dematerializes the two accommodation wings, generating different yet unified reflections during the day and becoming a luminous block at night. In addition, there is the metal structure of the »greenhouse«, as well as other visible metallic parts, which transpose, through the clarity of their design, the idea of luminosity. Some correspondence is established between the harmonious, balanced design of the interior and the simple, coherent design of the building as a whole, which fits perfectly into its given space.

Moreover, the choice of materials contributes to the building's ecological credentials, because the polycarbonate envelope acts like a skin of perforated bricks, an insulating »garment« that provides internal thermal inertia, thereby perfectly complementing the passive insulation provided by

the transitional space of the greenhouse. Entirely neutral with respect to its environment, the polycarbonate façade allows a transition towards the street, the garden and the small wood behind the ensemble, while the building's black-concrete base anchors it in the ground and links it to the asphalt, the street and the neighbouring structures.

The architectural approach, which consisted in wrapping the building in a simple membrane just a few centimetres thick, speaks to a paradigm shift in architecture these past few years, the monolithic, massive and structural having given way to an architecture of the envelope, of mono-materiality even, reduced to a simple interface between interior and exterior. The idea of the »wall« is thus challenged, this multifunctional polycarbonate membrane not only protecting and insulating the interior but also bringing extra light. It is also transitional in character, to the extent that the cladding can be changed after a certain time – the possibility of evolution is thus »inscribed« in the architectural concept.

The Blériot building therefore goes beyond the simple requirements of the social-housing block, which is nearly always subject to stringent budget restrictions (for Blériot the price per square metre did exceed euros 1,300) and legislation that discourages architectural invention. This then is the real strength of a project whose approach completely changes the way architects, social-housing operators and developers envisage this type of programme and, in consequence, the status of social housing itself.

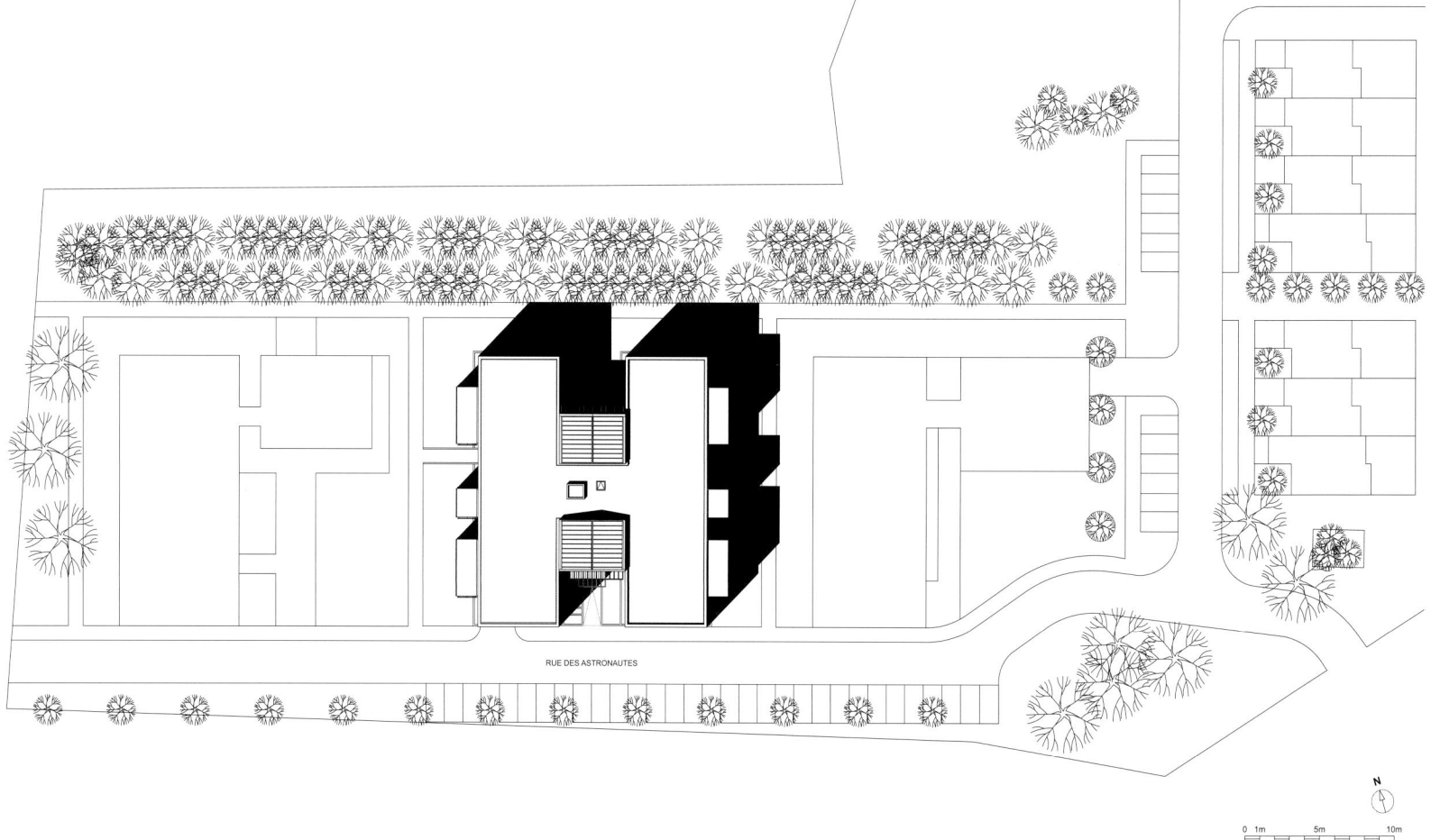

RUE DES ASTRONAUTES

0 1m   5m   10m

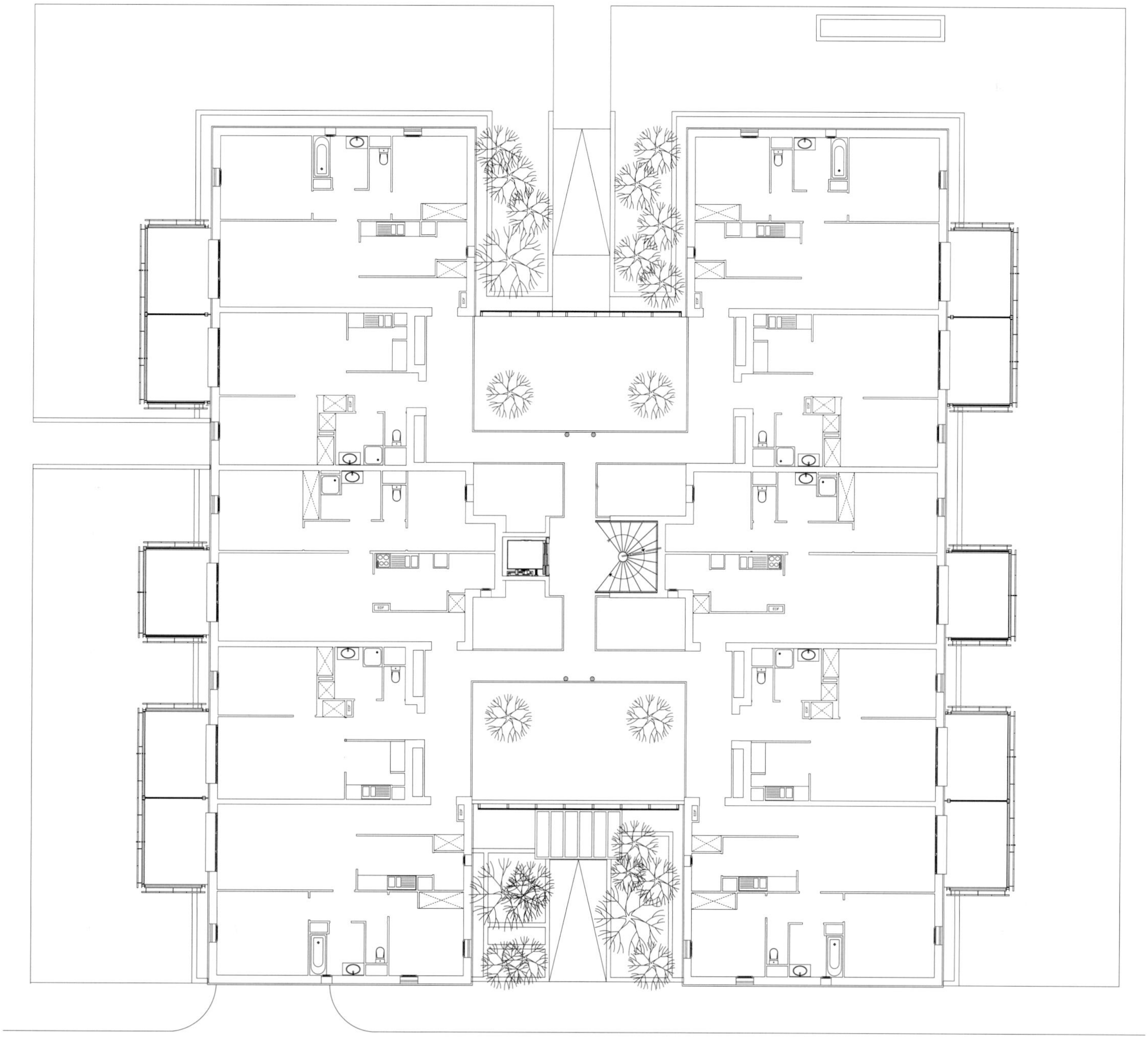

Résidence Cour Line Porcher, Saint-Pierre-des-Corps, Indre-et-Loire, 2009–13

Located near the town hall and library, both built by Barrier in 1988–96, the Line Porcher housing block is an essential component in the redevelopment of central Saint-Pierre-des-Corps, designed in continuity with the public buildings and taking into account the heritage aspect of the zone. Not only does this operation prolong an existing facility, it also creates a new point of urban and architectural identification in the town centre, which one might call »city block urbanism«: instead of being treated as a mere urban fragment defined by certain streets, the city block becomes an urban composition unto itself, an approach that is particularly evident in the relationship created with the new garden, whose planting is almost Mediterranean. In this sense, the apartment building is intended as a »wall« or »backdrop« creating a frame, or even a stage set, for the garden and this part of the centre.

Even if, due its compact volume, its cadenced, repetitive articulation and its mono-materiality, the building seems monolithic, it nonetheless has a lightness to its appearance thanks to its external envelope in polycarbonate (Danpalon/Everlite), which transforms it into an architecture of light. Conceived like a garment wrapping all-round the volume, without an apparent fixing structure to disturb the homogeneity, the façade cladding de-materializes the block. Moreover, with their double-aspect through planning, the apartments are also filled with light.

The exterior's appearance of massiveness is further diminished by the two stairwells, which divide up the block into several units, as well as by the pulling back of the final floor. This aspect of the building also bears witness to another particularity: each component and each volume expresses its function through its materials and form. While the main block is clad in polycarbonate, purely functional parts such as staircases or the attic floor are differentiated by their white-metal envelope. This logic allows the building's street façade to be »read«, since served and servant spaces are dissociated.

Lifted up off the ground to protect the dwellings from eventual flooding, the façade takes this principle one step further through its dynamic, almost kinetic composition, with balustrades, brise-soleils and corrugated-steel awnings that create lively plays of light and shadow and draw graphic lines across the elevation. The corrugated sheet metal also recalls the market-garden tradition of Saint-Pierre-des-Corps, a reference found, even if in rather abstract form, in the three garden sheds (also in corrugated steel) that stand on the terraces of the level-one apartments. Indeed, it is thanks to these small volumes that the compact form of the block dissolves, since they have been disposed irregularly, sometimes extending beyond the limit of the terrace, at others displaying different types of doors and windows.

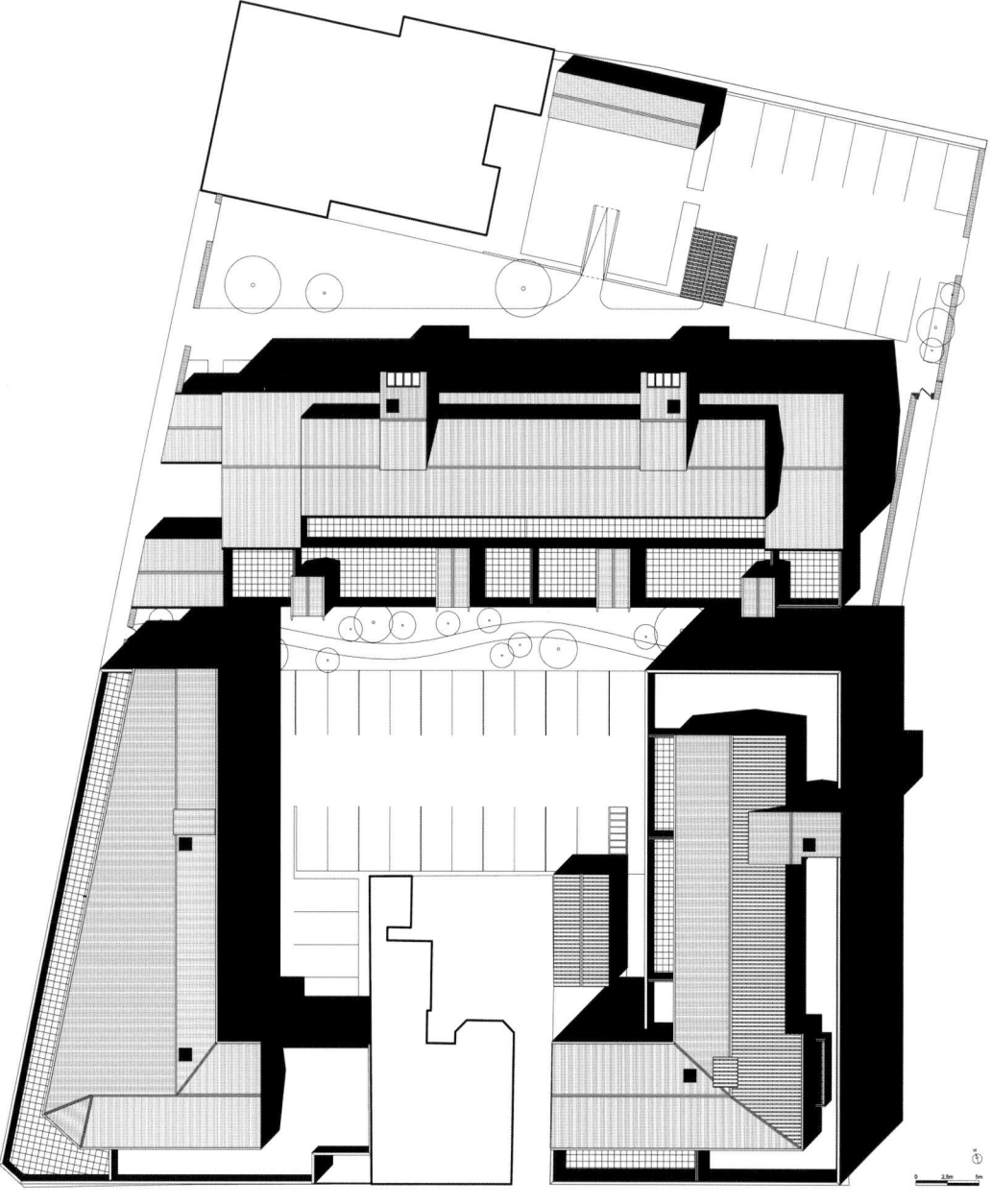

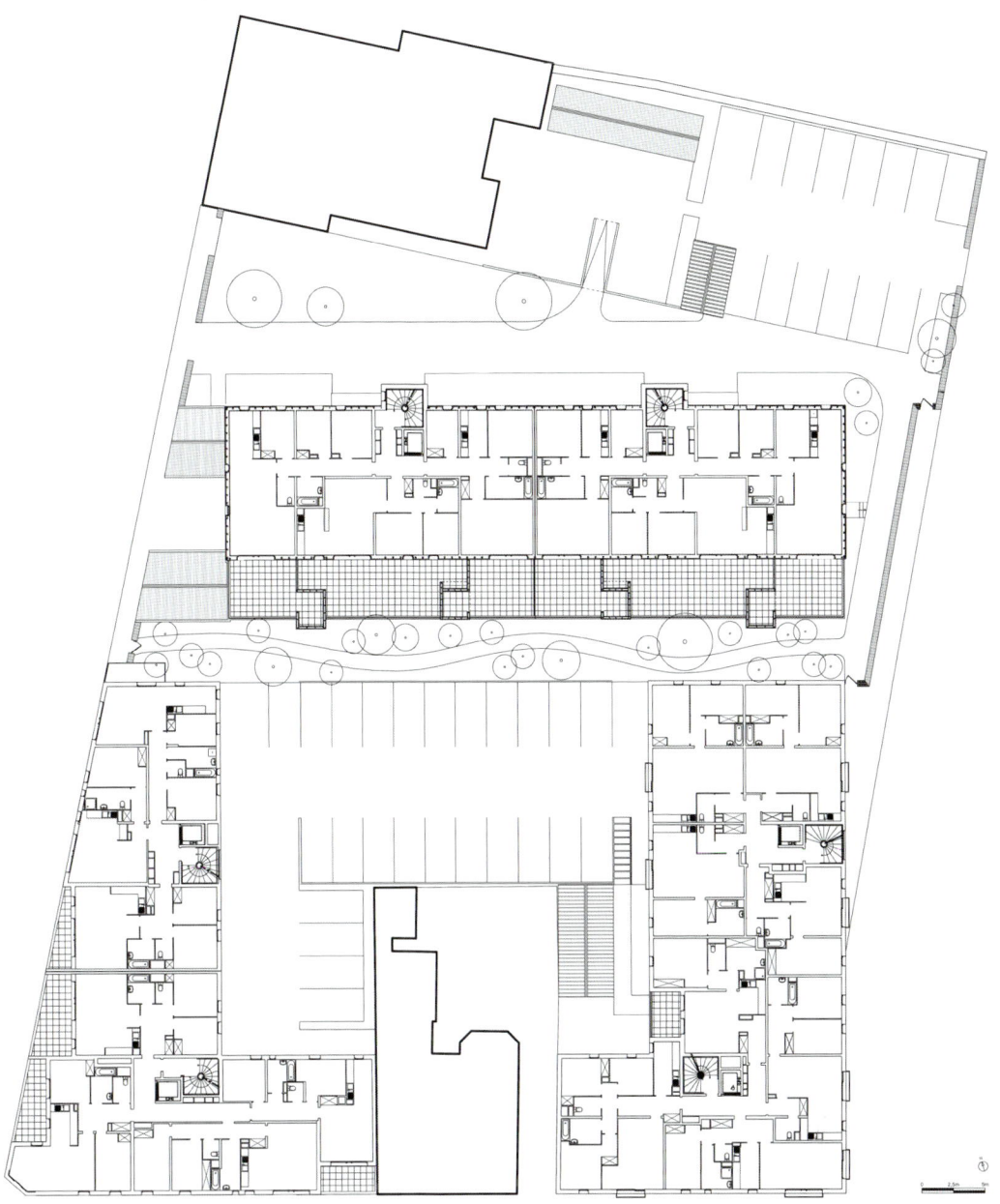

1. Site plan.
2. Standard-floor plan.
3. Façade overlooking the public garden.

4. South façade with private terraces.
5. North façade facing the street.

Résidence Bonne Garde, Nantes, Loire-Atlantique, 2008–14

The Bonne Garde social-housing complex is part of a vast operation of urban regeneration in the Clos-Toreau and Joliot Curie neighbourhoods of southern Nantes, which are also the entry point to the city. Built in 1972/73 on former agricultural land, the Clos-Toreau was the last big modernist housing estate in Nantes, located close to a historic site dating back to the 19th century, the Hôpital Saint-Jacques.

In June 2005, after a meeting of the various local authorities, the City of Nantes launched the Clos-Toreau operation, not only to enhance and renovate the enormous social-housing estate but also to regenerate the urban zones in its immediate vicinity. The transformation of this »chunk« of urbanity includes a reconfiguration of the public spaces, in particular the creation of a soft-transportation route, as well as densification, five plots being earmarked for construction, among them Bonne Garde.

Located at the far end of the neighbourhood, the site was formerly home to the regional blood-transfusion centre, part of the now-demolished hospital. Commissioned by Nantes Habitat (a social-housing operator owned by the city), the project comprises 44 dwellings: eight town houses with individual access and three five-storey apartment blocks, with just three flats per standard floor. Built along the Rue de Bonne-Garde, with a comb-like plan opening towards the heart of the plot, the ensemble comprises three distinct blocks, while on the street a succession of small blocks placed in front re-establishes a townhouse scale, a gradation of different heights that links the development to the road. Another street, internal this time and corresponding almost exactly to the external one, runs through the entire ensemble, creating a fluid plan that allows access to be easily understood.

Since the ambition was to reconcile architecture with the city, Barrier's Bonne Garde development seeks a truly urban form that borrows from town-planning theories developed by French architects such as Bernard Huet in the 1980s. Architecture must submit to the rules of the city, so at Bonne Garde Barrier sought to stitch the urban fabric back together with units and fragments that create a form of continuity. This notion of urban architecture is also expressed in the generosity of public, semi-public and private spaces, the Bonne Garde ensemble featuring a whole palette of shared spaces and convivial gardens, somewhere between the fully public and the entirely individual. At the same time, the balconies hidden behind climbing plants allow all the residents to enjoy a totally private outside space.

The internal street is a place of communication and encounter that provides access to all the houses and apartment buildings as well as the outside private spaces. The very fluid design of the shared spaces is all the more important in that the project seeks to promote social mixing. The general composition, with its organic simplicity, ensures that every dwelling is at least double aspect, with plentiful sunshine and multiple views out onto the surroundings, while the gardens have been laid out in terraces in order to deal with the slightly sloping terrain, which they balance out visually.

Though the general dispositions of the project allow the creation of very diverse and truly urban spaces, it is through formal features that the idea of »redesigning the city« is achieved: the gradation of volumes towards the street, which go from a vertical mass to more horizontal lines, is one expression of this. The ensemble is thus designed to ensure a continuity between it and the evolving environment, great attention being paid to the approaches and the design of the public spaces, like, for example, the corners, which take on the curve of the street. In addition, the silhouette of the ensemble was conceived so as to make it instantly recognisable within the reconfigured neighbourhood, setting in play a series of balanced contrasts: a black-clad vertical mass is matched by a band of white volumes, with the alternating solid and void of the vertical volumes corresponding to the alternating series of white blocks. All the components – railings and roof balustrades, the tensed cables of the balconies, the tightly cadenced staircase windows, the projecting and retreating façade components – bear witness to Barrier's constant preoccupation with designing every detail so as to ensure harmony and continuity between all the parts that go to make up the whole.

This emphasis on formal qualities is complemented by the technical choices with respect to structure and insulation, for example the façade cladding in Myral (a double skin in black-lacquered corrugated aluminium), which not only ensures thermal insulation from outside but also emphasizes the detailed, graphic qualities of the architecture, harmonizing with all the rest to form a new urban sector.

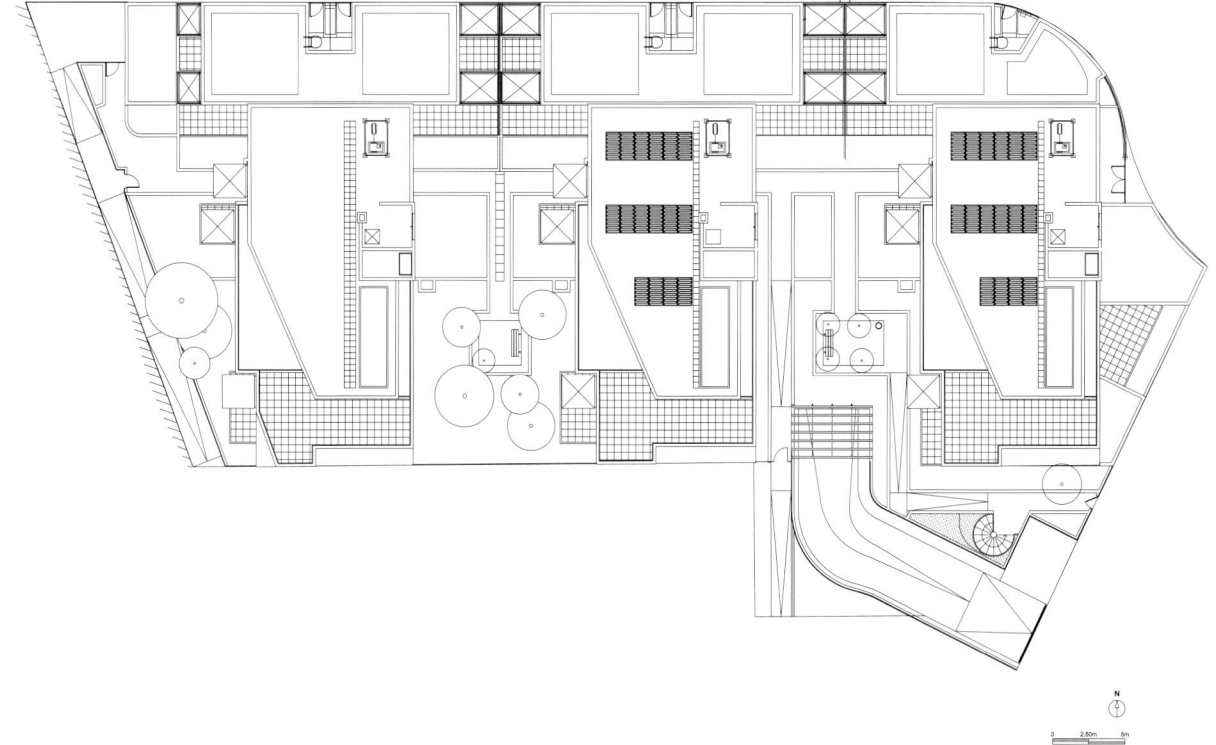

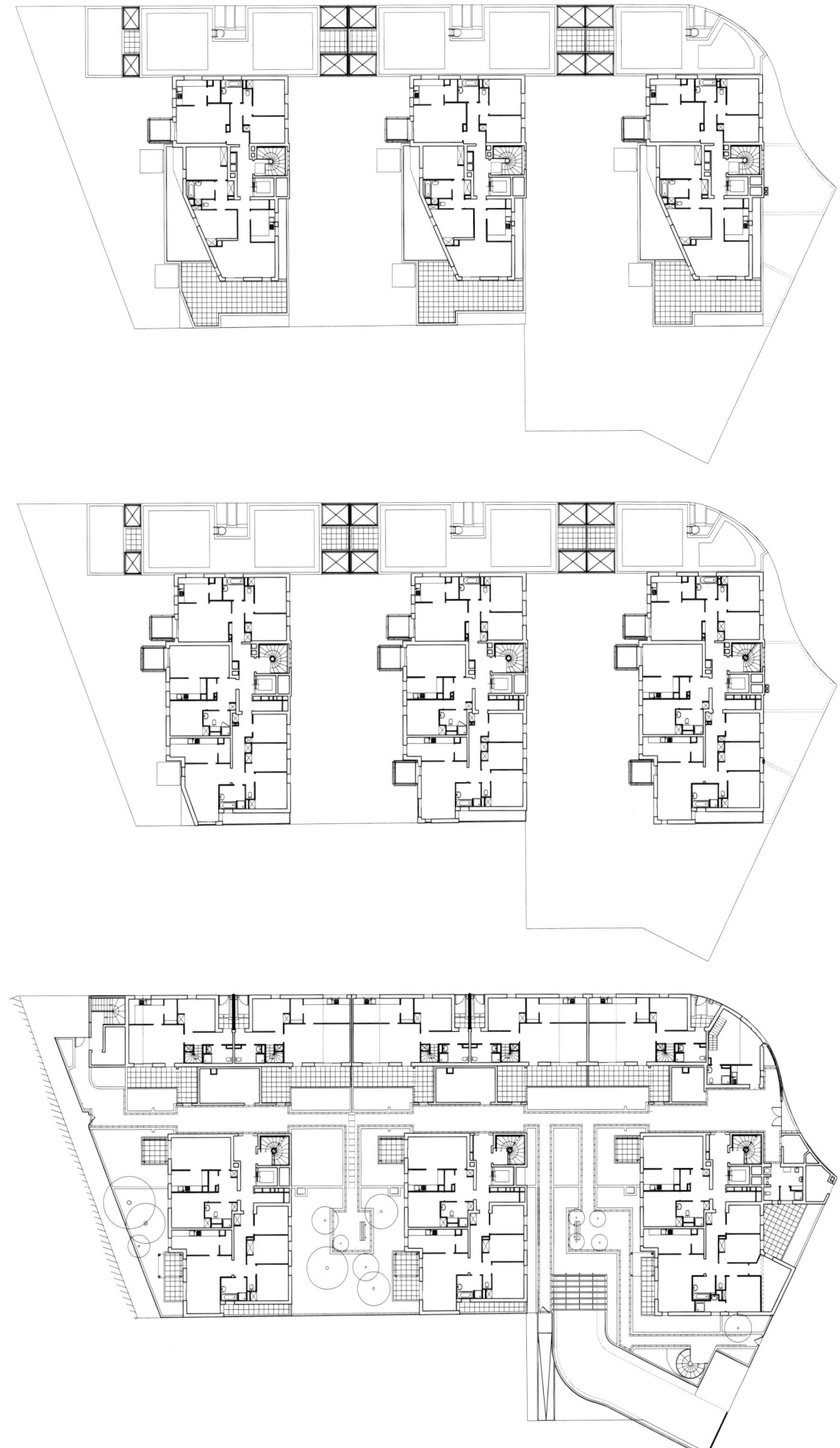

1. Roof plan.
2. Attic-floor plan.
3. Standard-floor plan.
4. Ground-floor plan.

5. General view across the gardens.
6. Interplay of the façades.
7. Corner treatment at the entrance to the street.

Jacques Decour development at the Monconseil eco-neighbourhood, Tours, Indre-et-Loire, 2008–16

Located in the new Monconseil eco-neighbourhood in Tours, the Jacques Decour operation comprises 46 dwellings divided into town houses, a small apartment building and intermediary housing. Ongoing since 2006, and master-planned by Eva Samuel Architects and Urbanists, Monconseil is among the largest urban projects in Tours, constituting a new centre to the north of the city. With an emphasis on quality of space and atmosphere, varying densities, and a mixed programme, it unites all the ingredients needed to develop highly urbane architecture.

Lined up along the Rue Jacques Decour, Les Florentines (realized for Tours Habitat) and Côté Jardin (developed for Touraine Logements) form a closed urban space that acts as an interface with the neighbouring suburban housing. Characterized by a play of different heights and volumes, the ensemble creates varied spatial tensions that diversify and animate the enfilade of dwelling units. Accentuating this diversity are the project's specific form, its compact and cubic volumes, the particular treatment of corners and entrances and a sort of outgrowth in the form of a trapezoid balcony, all of which bring a particular identity to these new little particuliers tourangeaux (a traditional type of single-family house typical of the region).

Alternation and continuity are thus the overriding themes of this operation, as can be seen in the architectural design, with façades that rise from a grey-concrete base and comprise strips of wood like half-timbering, a nod to local architectural traditions. The use of a single material and a nuanced single colour – recurring tropes in Barrier's work – create visual homogeneity, but repetition is avoided since each dwelling is personalized and each house has »its« façade. This is due in particular to the attention paid to the modularity of the cladding and the handling of its details, but also to a variation in the colour of the wooden strips, the rhythm of the composition, and the placing of fenestration.

The small apartment block near the central square displays other, equally unexpected variations through the addition of different white-lacquered metal structures, in particular the enormous balconies, the large external stairway, which is planted, and the second-floor winter garden, whose form is borrowed from the archetypal greenhouse. This attention to architectural quality is naturally found inside the dwellings, which vary from three to five bedrooms and whose average size is 83 m². Even if the houses are lined up in a serried row, the layout is organized in such a manner that different ways of occupying them are possible, all the while respecting privacy both within the household and with regard to neighbours.

On each of the plots, which measure between 200 and 300 m², an interweaving of spaces ensures a fluid relationship between inside and out: at the front, there is a small covered entrance court that acts as a transitional space between the street and the house; at the rear, a terrace, a garden and a garden shed, where tools can be kept for cultivating the shared kitchen garden. By echoing the architectural language of the house itself, each little shed reinforces the homogeneity of the ensemble.

Given that the dwelling units vary between two and three storeys and contain, depending on their size, one or two apartments, the occupants of the upper floors enjoy a private terrace that directly prolongs their accommodation. Inside, the generously glazed south-facing bays bring not only abundant light and views but also – and this is especially important for the smaller apartments – the impression of extra space.

1. North elevations facing the Rue Jacques Decour.
2. South elevations with the private gardens.
3. General plan.
4. »Côté jardin«. North elevations.
5. »Côté jardin«. South elevations.
6. »Côté jardin«. Upper-floor plan.
7. »Côté jardin«. Ground-floor plan

8. »Les Florentines«. North elevations.
9. »Les Florentines«. South elevations.
10. »Les Florentines«. Upper-floor plan.
11. »Les Florentines«. Ground-floor plan.

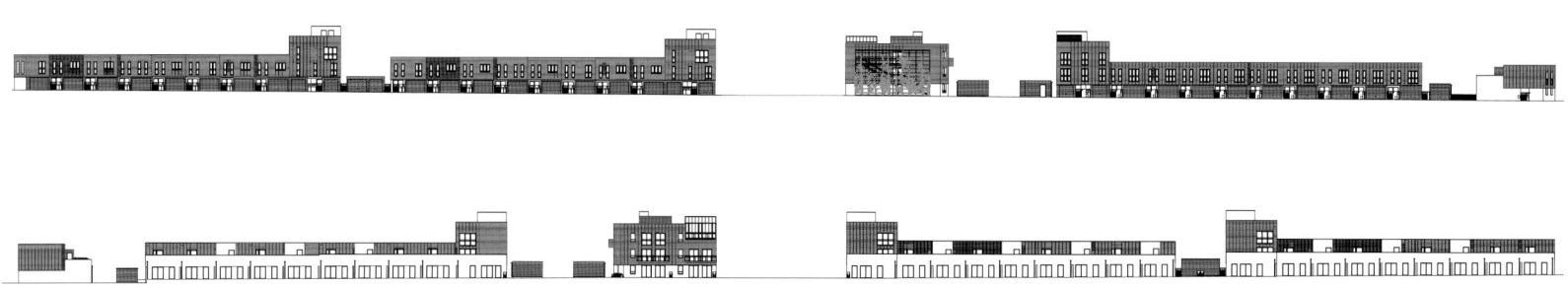

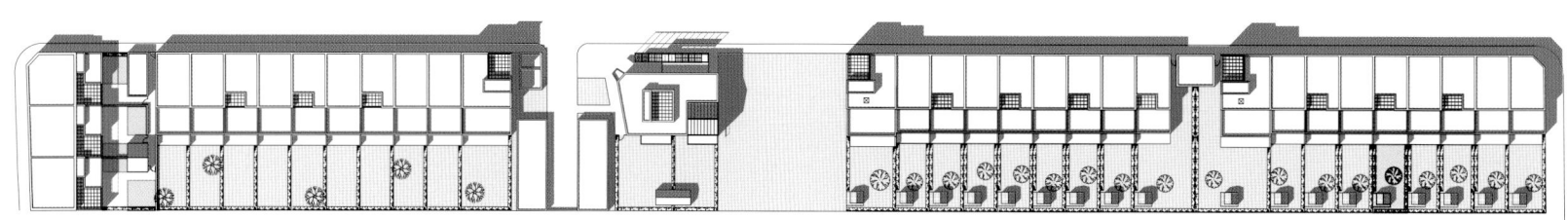

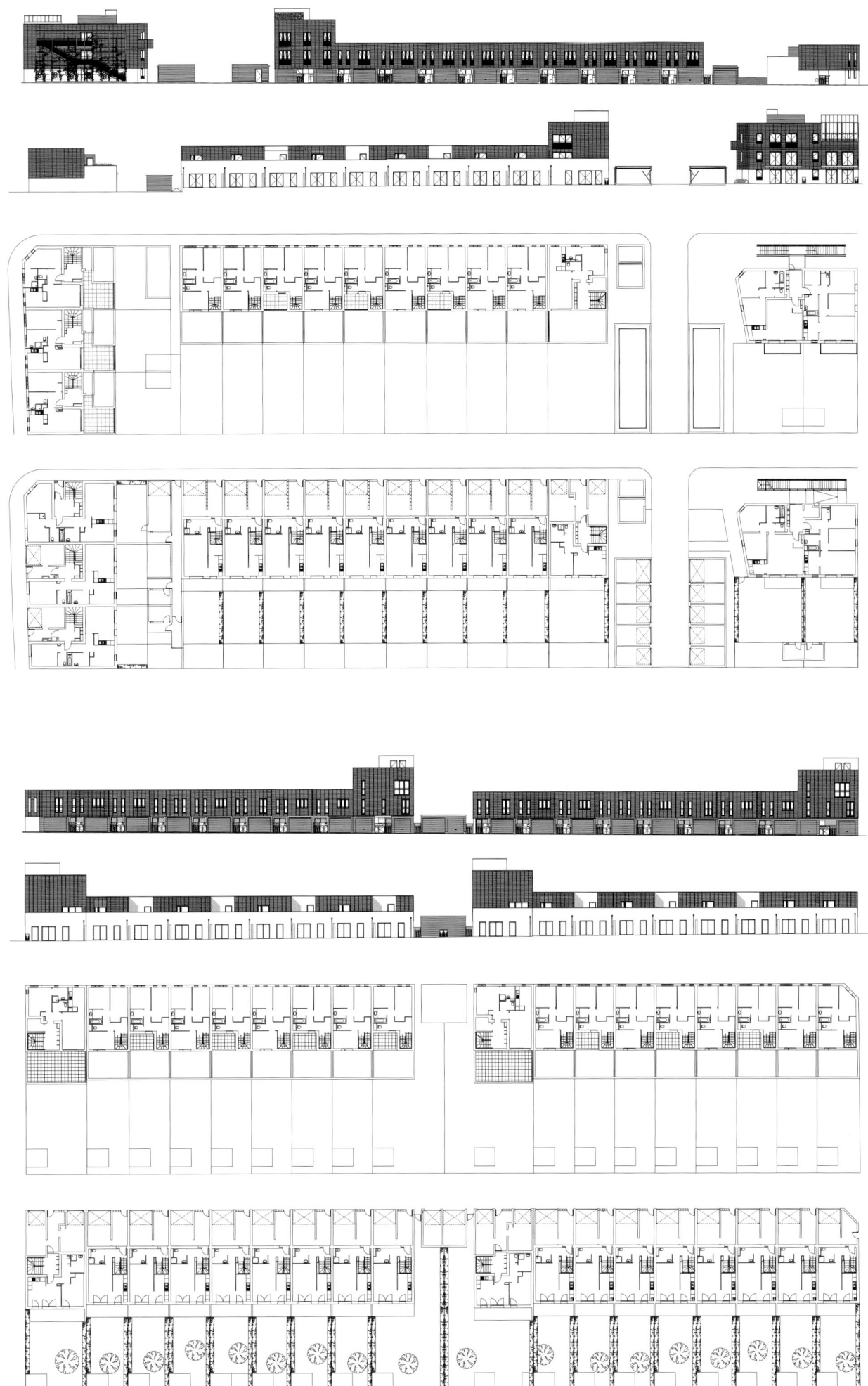

12. »Côté jardin«. South façade.
13. »Côté jardin«. East façade facing the public space and north façade facing the Rue Jacques Decour.
14. »Les Florentines«. South façades.

Résidence Les 3 rives, Rennes, Ille-et-Vilaine, 2004–07

Located in the Bourg-l'Évêque/La Touche/Moulin du Comte area of Rennes, Les 3 rives is part of a huge urban-regeneration operation begun in the early 1990s by the architect-urbanist Alexandre Chemetoff, particularly in the Du Mail and De la Mabilais redevelopment zones. Working hand in hand with 70 different architecture offices to produce 3,300 dwellings and 8,200 m² of shops and offices on a site of over 23 ha, Chemetoff set out to ensure a logical relationship between the new buildings, the existing architectural fabric and the topography on the banks of the river Vilaine.

An eight-storey block containing 45 apartments, Les 3 rives is sited on the Quai Ouest plot alongside the 800 m-long by 50 m-wide Mail François-Mitterrand, which, initially destined to be a car park, was landscaped in 2015 as an urban promenade. Through its compact massing – a U-shaped block built around a courtyard – Les 3 rives responds to a neighbouring building (Chouzenoux, Architecte 2003), setting up a dialogue that is expressed through volume, string courses and the tripartite division into a base, a main elevation, and an attic, on top of which rises an autonomous structure that takes the form of a house on the roof. This composition conformed to Chemetoff & Associés's guidelines, which sought to compensate for heights and volumes that might have ap-

peared too vertical and massive through the use of top-floor step-backs, thereby establishing a median height among the different apartment buildings. For the Quai Ouest site, Chemetoff specified that buildings of identical volume should stand opposite each other but that each should be designed by a different architect, to produce a musical effect of variations on the same theme. While Chouzenoux's building responded to the brief with a compact, almost monumental mass, Barrier opted for something much lighter, surmounting his double-height base with three main levels that feature long, wrap-around balconies on each side. In order to balance this main part of the building with the three-storey roof structures, Barrier linked the balconies with a metal structure that brings a vertical emphasis, thereby reducing the monolithic character of the roof storeys. To make the latter read as an attic, Barrier clad them in zinc, something of a leitmotiv in Chemetoff's development zones in Rennes.

Complementing the dark metal above, the three middle floors sport white façades and alternating glass and fritted balcony panels that ensure both a more airy elevation and privacy for the occupants. The graphic lines of the fritting reproduce a freehand drawing of motifs that are similar to curved ironwork, cadencing the façades through their dynamic form and bringing visual unity through their repetition. This effect of movement is echoed inside by the spacious, fluid plans of the individual apartments.

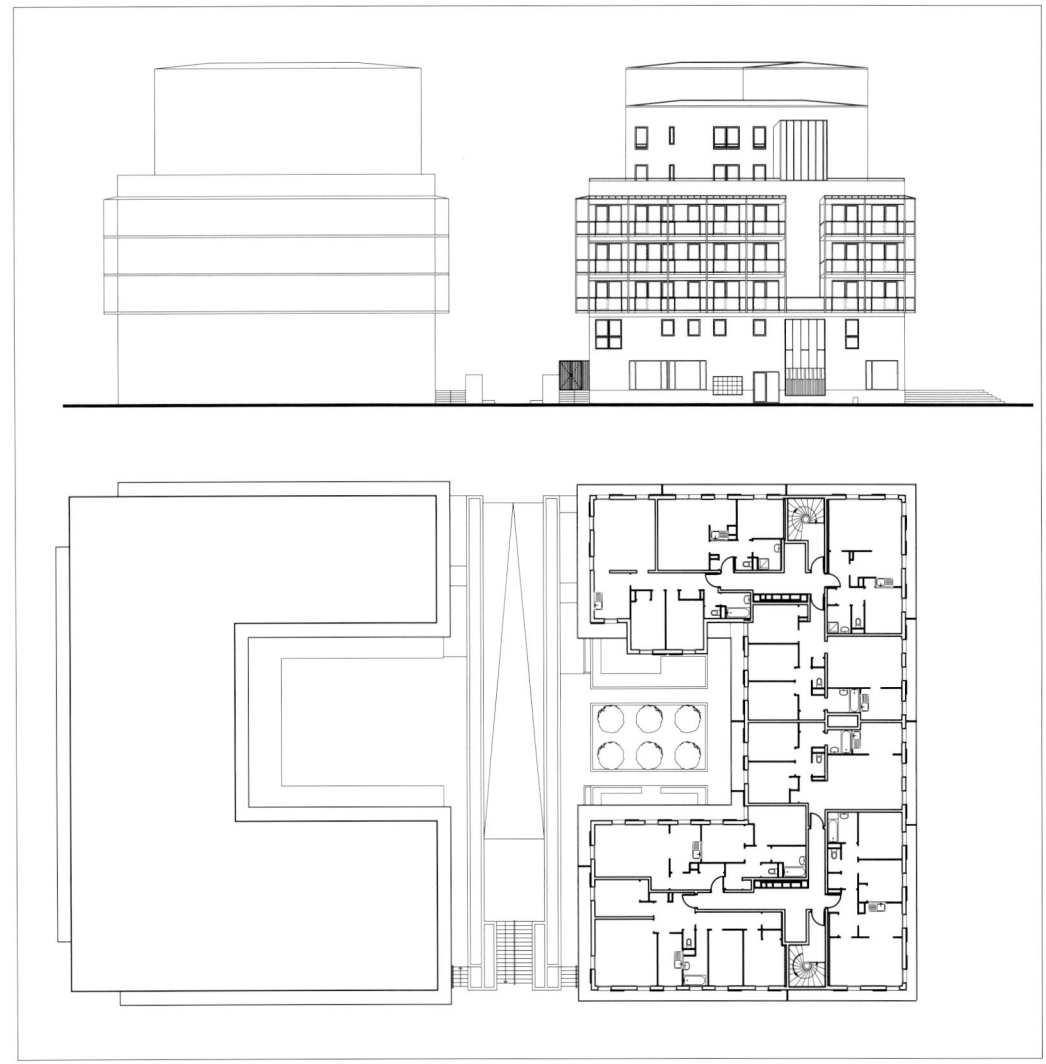

1. Floor plan and elevation.
2. View from the public space.
3. Detailed view of the façade.

pp. 84, 85
4. The interior patio.
5. The building in the urban context.

Zac Libera housing, Colombelles, Calvados, 2010–14

Located in the Libera redevelopment zone in Colombelles, this multi-site operation comprises 47 social-sector rental dwellings: 14 detached houses and an apartment building of 33 units. Launched in 2007, Libera is one of the first urbanization projects undertaken at the erstwhile SMN (Société Métallurgique de Normandie) industrial complex and concerns an area formerly home to the factory's sports grounds and garages. Even if the SMN site is still strongly marked by its industrial past, this sector had been entirely cleared, with only a concrete water tower to remind the visitor of its previous use. Besides this piece of infrastructure, there were no cues, landmarks or even trees to work with, setting the challenge of turning this tabula rasa into a new urban neighbourhood of housing and public amenities.

As demonstrated by many of his projects, one of the characteristics of Barrier's creative approach is to design truly urban ensembles when transforming inner-city or suburban sites that are often lacking in any urban or architectural coherence, making of them new neighbourhoods with landmarks at different scales. For him, urban evolution is not just a succession of different temporal strata but also a collage, an interweaving – a cohabitation even – of many different possibilities that allow the urban composition to be continued.

The 14 small rental houses, divided between two sites and lined up along a street, form a unit unto themselves. Colour differences, strongly underlined by the fact that each house is monochrome, as well as a variety of alternating volumes, ensure diversity within this very modest operation. The second housing group differs from the first by placing greater emphasis on the masonry base and the timber-framed upper floor.

The third part of the project, an apartment block of 33 dwellings, plays the role of an urban landmark, bringing a new identity to the site that allows it to be identified from afar, particularly by drivers on the nearby highway. A mono-block crowned with three distinct volumes, it acts as an autonomous object, though without appearing ostentatious, its monolithic form moulding space in this new neighbourhood and forming a »backdrop« or »architectural screen« that closes and circumscribes a place hitherto devoid of any identity or coherence. This impression is further underlined by the building's 4 m setback from the plot's northern limit, thereby creating a transitional space between the street and the dwellings.

This urban quality is also to be found in the handling of shared spaces and the layout of the apartments, all of which feature through north–south accommodation that enjoys abundant daylight and views out over the neighbourhood, some dwellings acting almost like urban »observatories«. Moreover, the four-bedroom apartments benefit from roof terraces, completing the open, permeable nature of the architecture, whose formal qualities owe much to the three, clearly marked entrances that access all the dwellings. These volumes stand out through the choice of materials and colours: a white-rendered ground floor, upper levels clad in either dark or galvanized aluminium, and roofing in steel that matches the colour of the façades.

The three interventions at Colombelles clearly demonstrate that there are many ways of renewing modest, domestic typologies while continuing the urban composition.

1. Entrances and vertical services on the north side.
2. Attic-floor plan.
3. First-floor plan.
4. Ground-floor plan.

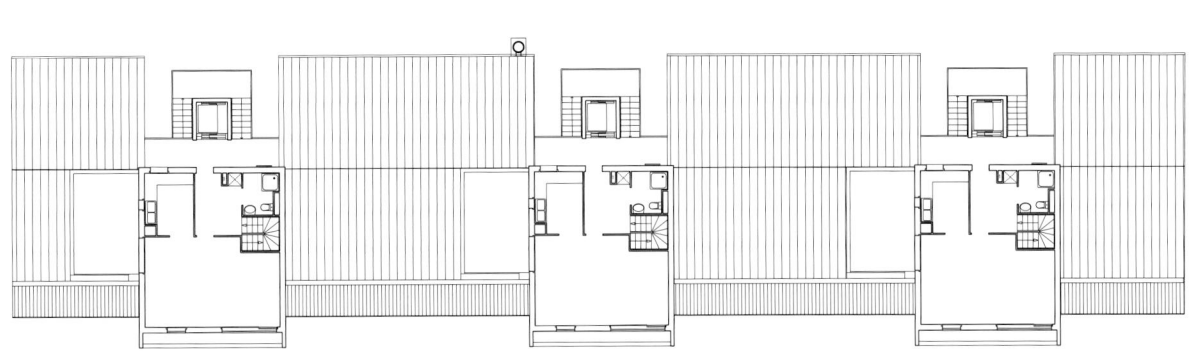

NIVEAU ATTIQUE

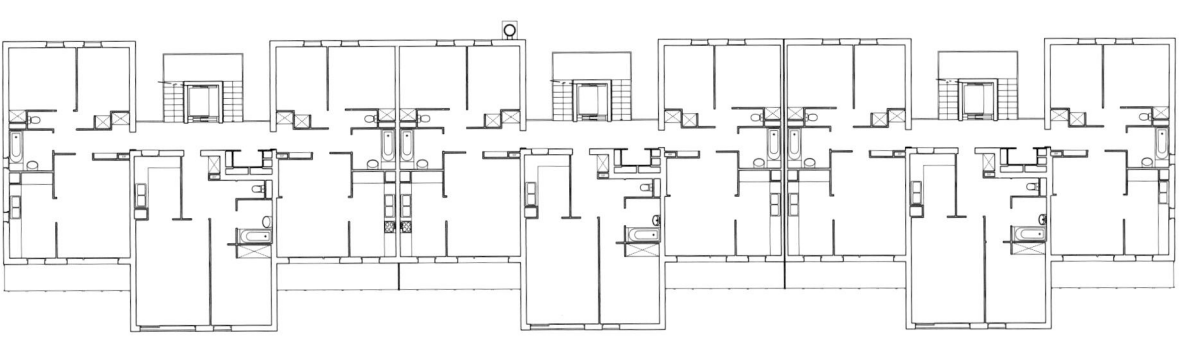

NIVEAU R+1

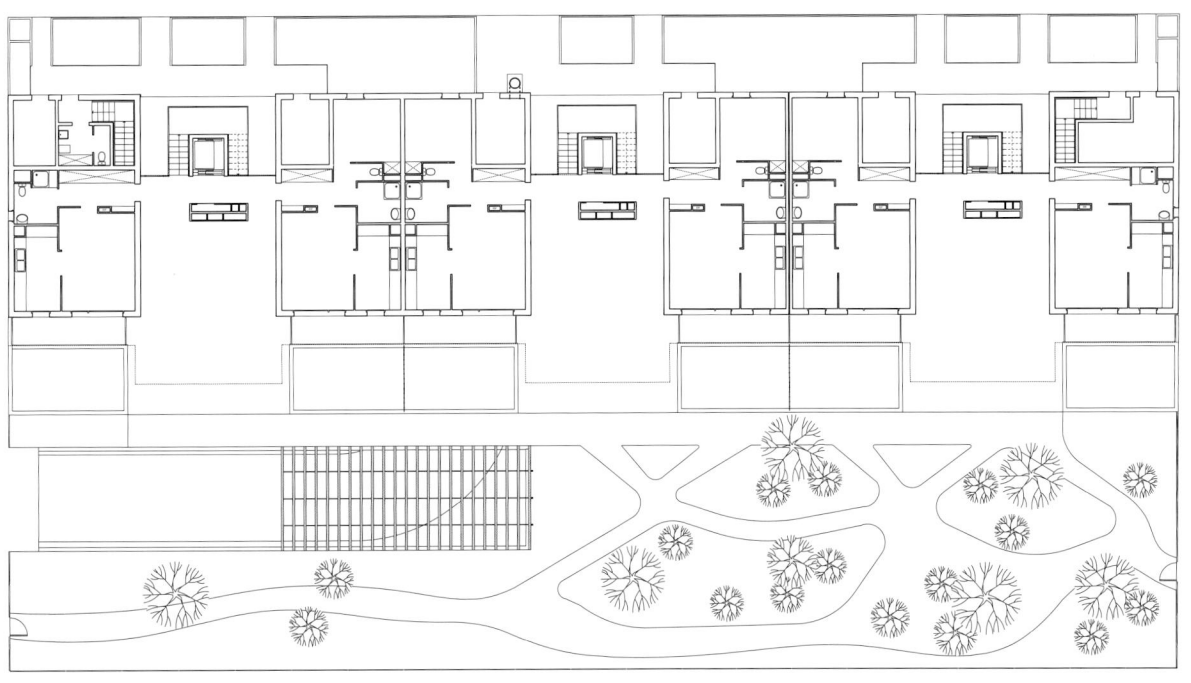

NIVEAU RDC

5. South façade.
6. View of the garden.

Résidence Aquarelle, Chantepie, Ille-et-Vilaine, 2006–08

Located in the Rives du Blosne development area in Chantepie, which is part of Rennes Métropole, the Aquarelle housing complex stands at the southwestern entrance to this new neighbourhood, close to the Touche Annette sector. The 46 social-sector dwellings are divided among three buildings: a principal structure whose longitudinal form is oriented east–west, and two other blocks located to the south and north of the plot. Standing on a semi-sunken car park and rising four stories plus a final attic level, the buildings form a U-shaped composition around a central garden. This green open space is treated as a series of four ascending levels that ensure the transition between grade and the height of the car park, allowing the latter to be naturally lit. Each level is planted with different species according to an increasing rate of humidity (grasses, bamboo, reeds).

Two vertical metallic structures rise from the garden, thereby framing a backdrop when viewed from the new boulevard. Indeed it was with the goal of creating a new urban composition that the operation was planned as a focal point in the perspective as seen from the thoroughfare. These two metal totems, up which rise climbing plants (honeysuckle), are illuminated at night, while their bases house the pumps that distribute rain- and grey water around the garden. Functioning like sculptures or design objects, the totems are characteristic of Barrier's urban and architectural approach.

Rising from a common base, the three buildings alternate different types of façade finish: white render, sang-de-boeuf timber cladding and, on the attic storeys, patinated zinc. Furthermore, a certain number of features ensure that the ensemble blends into its immediate environment, tempering the prevailing rectangularity and ensuring a transition in scale. Because the plot is located in the axis of the boulevard, the complex acts as a theatrical composition, with a gradation of red and grey volumes framed by two white blocks, like entrance pavilions, and the garden as the stage itself. A third component takes the form of a footbridge leading to the internal street, which provides access to the entrance halls and centres the complex with respect to the existing street layout.

A relationship is established with the natural environment to the west thanks to trees and shrubs that have been planted in alignment with the existing green areas, while a footpath crosses the complex from north to south, thereby ensuring a visual perspective and linking the Rue du Pont-Bœuf to the pond at the northern edge of the site. In addition to these strong links to the natural environment, the complex includes planted terraces and other greenery. The sensation of an airy ensemble oriented towards the landscape is accentuated by the through accommodation and clear layout of the dwellings themselves.

For this rental programme, launched by the Rennes Métropole, Barrier sought, as so often in his work, bespoke solutions that would bring a unique character and quality of life to this social-housing ensemble.

1. Site plan plan.
2, 3. Elevations.
4. Ground-floor plan.

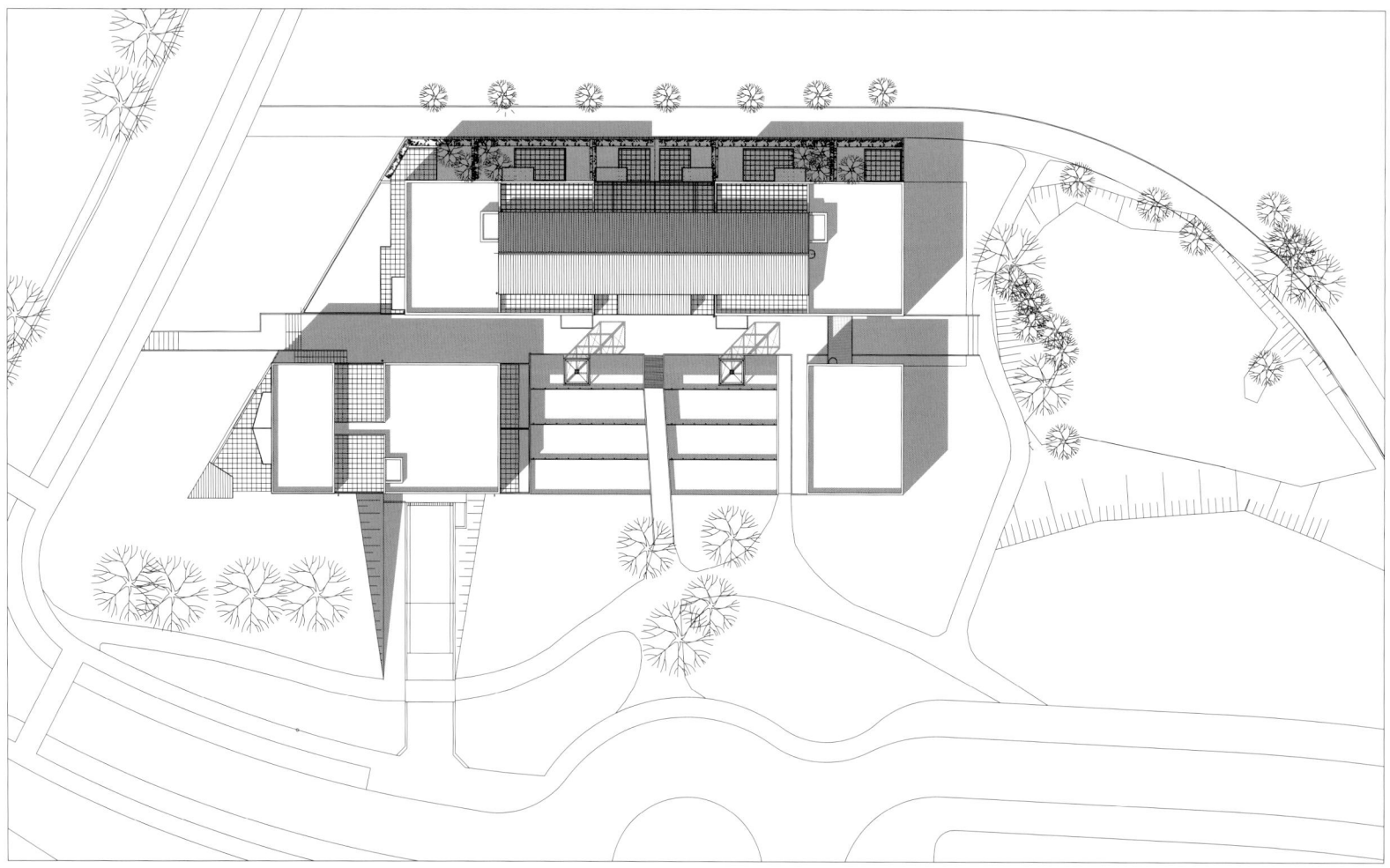

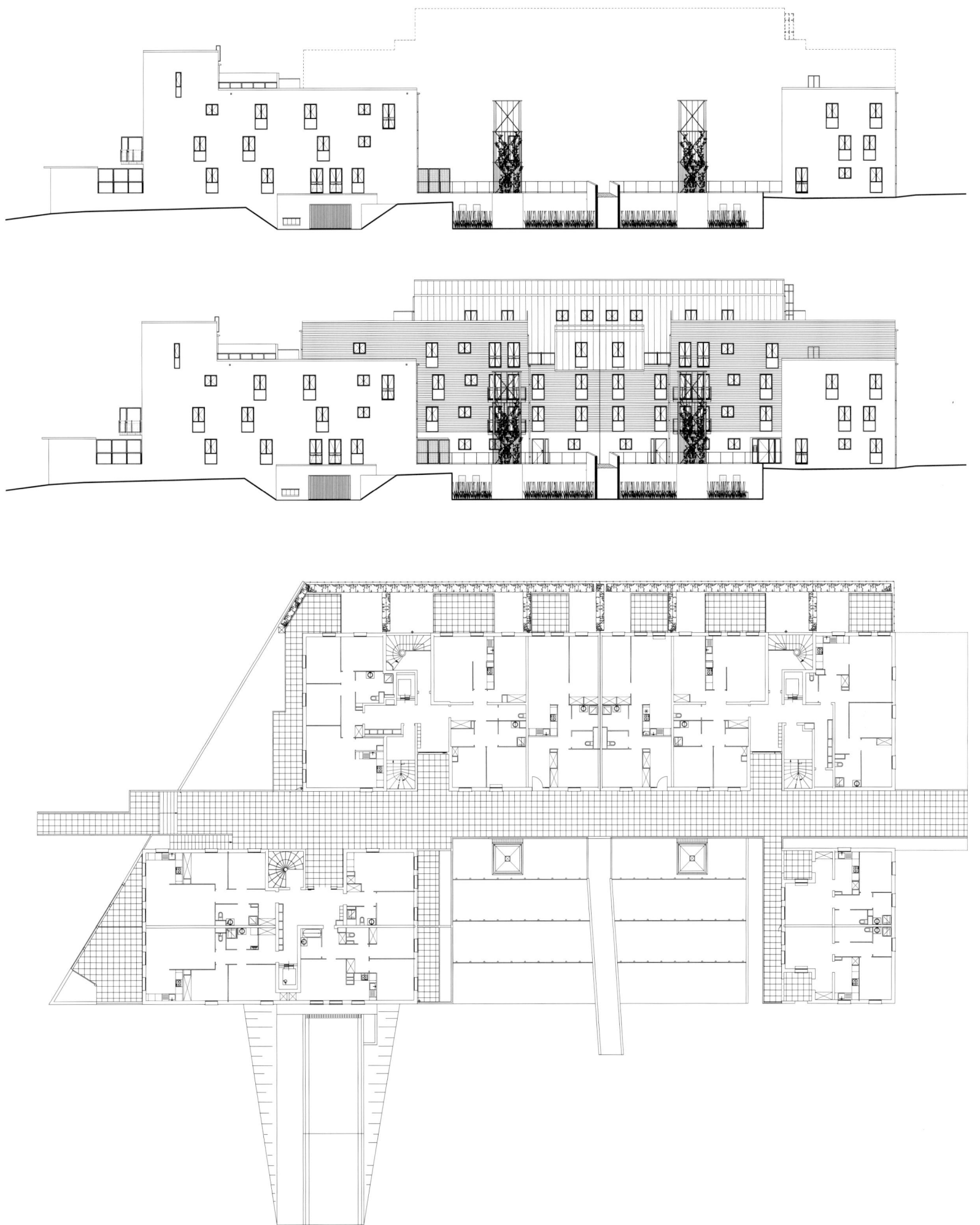

5. The residence facing the new avenue.
6. The entrance on the Rue du Pont-Bœuf.
7. The two totem structures.

Résidence Le Cristalium, Tours, Indre-et-Loire, 2012–15

Located in the Monconseil eco-neighbourhood in northern Tours, Le Cristalium comprises ground-floor retail units and 92 dwellings divided between four buildings laid out on a rectangular site. Three of the buildings respect the street line on the Rues Daniel-Mayer and Françoise-Giroud, while the fourth, at the heart of the plot, acts as a scenic »backdrop«. Despite its diverse offer, from social-sector rentals to market-price freeholds, the ensemble presents a formally coherent appearance that chimes with the scale and urban regulations of the neighbourhood. Nonetheless, each of the four buildings expresses its own particular identity through its architecture.

The corner building, where the two streets meet, stands out more than the others in its architectural approach, since the City of Tours and the architect-urbanist in charge of the eco-neighbourhood, Eva Samuel, wanted this block to rise three storeys higher than the other buildings on the avenue and so form an urban landmark at the scale of the area. To avoid an effect of over-monumental massiveness that might have seemed a little unbalanced with respect to the rest of the built fabric, Barrier designed a crystalline silhouette that, through its volume, angles and uniform envelope, recalls a facetted gemstone, which is what gave the ensemble its name. The impression of a block that has been carved and bevelled is reinforced by the fact that the windows, loggias and roof openings seem to have been drilled into this compact volume, creating different-sized white cavities. The form of the block, which resembles a parallelogram, results from a deformation of a rectangular plan adapted to the open angle formed by the two streets that access the site, with a three-storey roof whose volume dialogues with the distortion of the façade. All these inclined surfaces correspond to the building envelope as defined by the urban regulations governing the eco-neighbourhood. Finally, in order to ensure a balanced relationship between the three registers that are the base, the main elevation and the attic, the ground-floor features inclined angles that respond to those of the roof.

The building's compact, monolithic character is emphasized by the tobacco-coloured metal that clads both the façades and the roof and dialogues with another urban landmark within view of Le Cristalium, the Tours-Nord belfry (renovated by the architects Sophie Berthelier and Benoît Tribouillet, in 2009, the belfry features white-metal cladding on its elevations and roof that emphasize its verticality). Le Cristalium's external envelope also helps reduce energy consumption, since the Myral sandwich panels ensure a high level of insulation and the avoidance of thermal bridges, allowing the project to meet the demanding energy targets set for the neighbourhood.

On the three final floors, the building's unusual form influences the arrangement and spatial configuration of the dwellings, with certain spaces seeming as though they have been sculpted, their volumes dynamized by the play of inclined surfaces. These apartments are each very different from the others, but they all enjoy splendid views over the immediate neighbourhood and the city at large.

The large open area at the centre of the plot respects the urban design of the neighbourhood, with landscaping that creates a series of spaces in the spirit of a small public garden: a paved esplanade on the Rue Daniel-Meyer that opens onto greenery; and a small square on the Rue Françoise-Giroud, which is set in the axis of a large pergola at the foot of the lift shaft that rises like a totem at the garden's centre. Here, as so often in the Touraine, we find roses, laid out in a geometric design of off-set strips that ensure a transition from the mineral to the vegetal. The light structures of the walkways running along the apartment buildings' façades create a harmonious relationship between the urban architecture and the large green space, which features a fluid network of pathways accessing the entrances to each block and the ground-floor retail units.

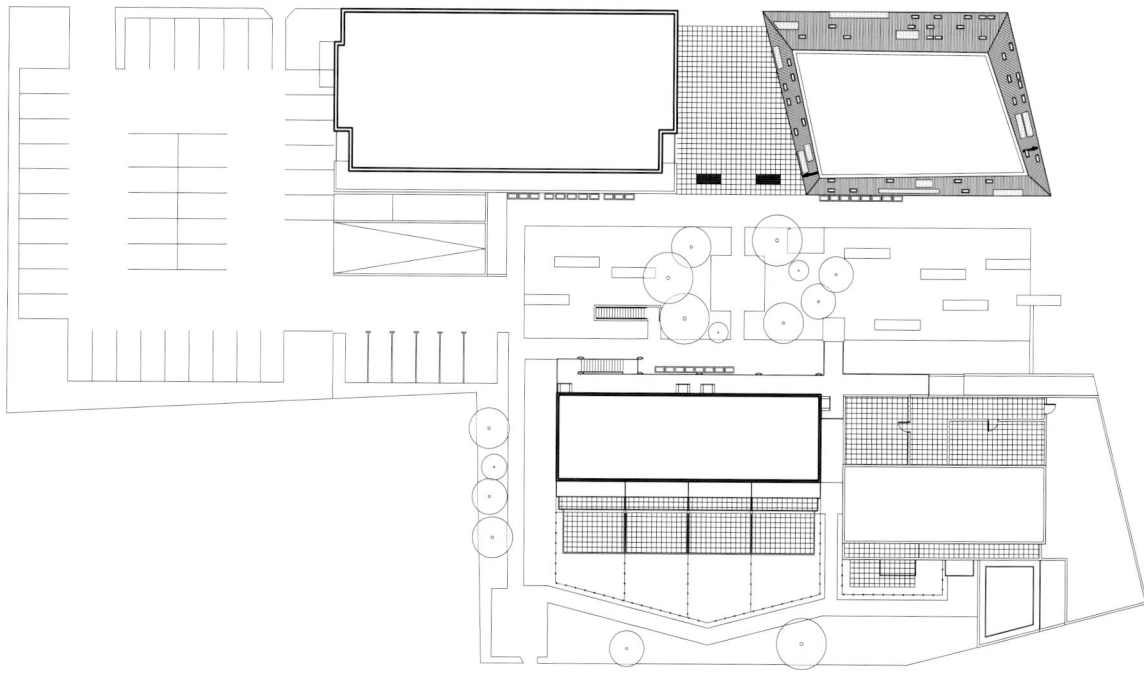

1. Site plan.
2. Standard-floor plan.

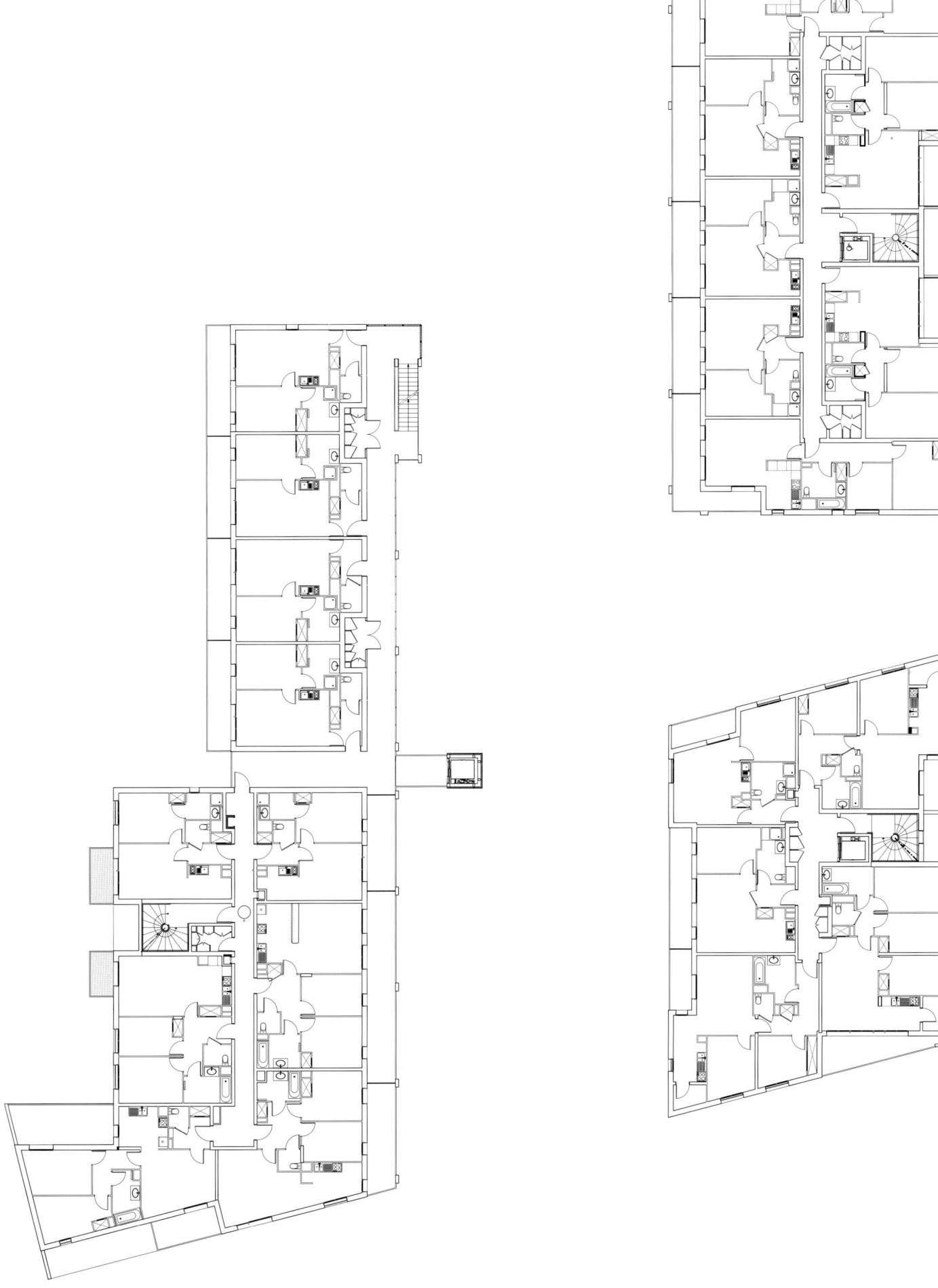

3, 4. Façades facing the Avenue Daniel Mayer.
façades.

Résidence Les Jardins Boileau, Saint-Pierre-des-Corps, Indre-et-Loire, 2010–15

Located on silty ground between the Rivers Loire and Cher, Saint-Pierre-des-Corps, like many other municipalities in the Loire Valley, is at risk of flooding. In order to find long-term solutions, Saint-Pierre has been selected as one of six French pilot boroughs – in light of this objective, every new architectural project must, according to the policy adopted by the municipality, »integrate flood risk into its design«. Among the potential solutions, raising buildings on pilotis, using particular materials and adopting specific spatial layouts will together create new typologies in response to this issue.

Barrier, who since the late 1980s has worked at Saint-Pierre-des-Corps as both an architect and urbanist, is well aware of the problem, seeking new solutions with each project, as his back catalogue clearly demonstrates. The Boileau apartment block is another chapter in his search for the creative potential in an apparent obstacle, its pertinence hailed in 2015 when it was selected as a finalist in the Grand Prix for development entitled »How can we build better on flood-prone sites?«

The 28-dwelling, four-storey complex was designed for a former market-garden site by the River Loire near the dyke. It follows the logic of market-garden structures, an important stratum in Saint-Pierre's history that accompanies the streets and alleyways running perpendicular to the avenue on which the block stands. Flood risk is taken into account in several ways. Firstly the footprint is kept small – just 10 % of the plot; secondly the elongated design revisits a typology that has been present in the region since construction of the Château de Chenonceau (early 16th century), namely the inhabited bridge; and thirdly the plan follows the regulations set forth in the Plan for Preventing Flood Risk, with parking for 23 cars in a semi-basement, a medical practice (radiology) raised 50 cm above grade, and dwellings placed beyond the maximum recorded flood level.

Lacquered-steel cladding helps limit flood damage, protects the external insulation and adds architectural distinction, its gentle corrugations unifying the roof, the end walls and the main elevations and becoming one with the galvanized-steel walkways. This mono-material approach creates a texture and a tactility, not only by reflecting the light in multiple facets, but also by producing a sort of scintillating vibration. Mono-materiality does not mean monotony, however, especially since the articulation of the façades (both the street and garden elevations) is characterized by a play of volumes and openings (balconies, windows, patios, pergolas) and solids and voids, as well as by a graphic arrangement of carefully designed contours. This impression of a simple formal variation is, in fact, the result of the building's plan, since the two sides of its median axis mirror each other, with double-aspect two- and three-bedroom apartments and duplex four-bed dwellings in the attic. The freedom found in the façade composition and the apartment layout is also present in the access structures, with stairs, walkways and footbridges displaying a graphic play of constructive lines that multiplies the sources of luminosity.

1. Site plan.
2–4. Standard-floor plan and duplex lower-level and duplex upper-level plans.

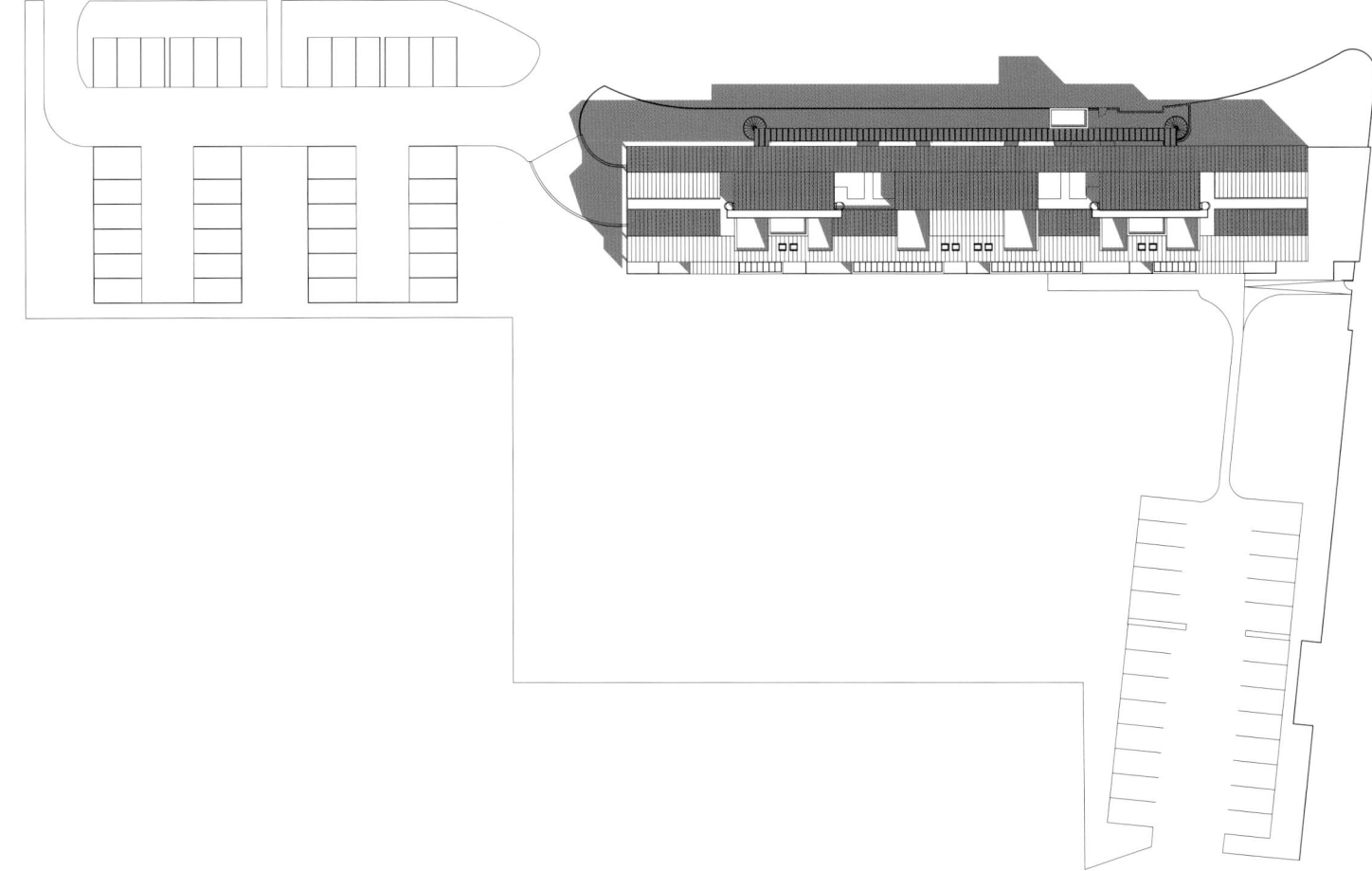

ETAGES COURANTS   DUPLEX NIVEAU BAS   DUPLEX NIVEAU HAUT

5. Façade facing the Rue Boileau.
6. Façade facing the private space.

Résidence Canopée, Saint-Pierre-des-Corps, Indre-et-Loire, 2020–

The project is part of a densification programme in an urban neighbourhood, one of the preferred solutions in the fight against sprawl. Such policies often involve a change of use or the rehabilitation of buildings that have become insalubrious, with priority placed on tall structures. The approach can also be accompanied by its opposite, namely a dedensification of the centre of the city block. In these zones, the introduction of new activities that were previously scattered encourages the process of densification. At Saint-Pierre-des-Corps, the development (currently being realized) not only provides an urban and architectural response to this question but also deals with pressing urban issues: transport, climate, environment, flood risk, the treatment of different scales in a neighbourhood and how to address the consequences of the COVID-19 epidemic.

Located in the centre of »old Saint-Pierre«, the site has had several lives over the course of its history, with several buildings that these past few years housed a laboratory. It will remain marked by a large building and a small late-19th-century house that will be kept, as well as a large pine tree. An elongated rectangle, the urban block will see the preserved buildings integrated with new structures that will encircle a vast interior courtyard. One of the project's particularities is the emphasis on soft transport, the dwellings being reached by footpaths from internal gardens with walkways for the upper floors. Bike sheds, cycle lanes, small private courtyards equipped with chargers for electric bicycles, as well as bike lifts

so you can bring your vehicle inside the home, are among the innovative features that demonstrate the many ways that soft transportation can be integrated architecturally into a collective-housing project.

Among other themes explored in this development is the importance of greenery, with specific architectural and landscape-design approaches that allowed grade-level green spaces to be increased from 894 m² to 1,027 m² despite a built footprint that has almost doubled. This apparent paradox was achieved by reducing parking and internal driveways by almost a third. The highlighting of the large pine, the creation of a generous interior park (a true oasis of fresh air planted with tall trees), the shrubberies that accompany the internal pedestrian route, the pergolas with their climbing plants, the planted terraces, the private gardens and the shared vegetable gardens all come together to provide a very varied vegetal palette that softly integrates the operation into the neighbourhood while creating interfaces and transitional zones with the neighbouring streets and buildings.

Climate requirements also determined the design of the 25 dwellings, with all the apartments, which range from three bedrooms to five, featuring through accommodation that is at the very least double aspect, with multiple aspects for the bigger flats. East–west and north–south orientation allows sun and shade to be varied according to season and the time of day, ensuring optimal comfort in both winter and summer. This is why the buildings are narrow, to allow natural ventilation and sunlight to penetrate right to the back each room. This architectural approach is further developed in the shady courtyard and the large

glazed bays with balconies. The outer façades, in contrast, are simpler and less open.

But the real particularity of this operation is to be found in its response to the risk of flooding and its adoption of the guidelines set out in the prevention plan. Bedrooms must be placed above the level of the highest known floodwaters, while the ground floor in new buildings must be reserved for parking. Where the older buildings were concerned, refuge spaces for the ground-floor dwellings had to be provided higher up. The original solution to this problem was to design cabins in the park that are linked to the apartments in question by staircases, an idea that will be applied to a dozen dwellings scattered throughout the different buildings on the site on different levels, up to the terraces. Even if the project was started before the COVID-19 lockdowns, the cabin becomes that extra room, the one that allows the dwelling to accommodate home working. These ten cabins are also a strong contributor to the project's architectural identity, which is already marked by the imbrication of volumes and the many roofs. By integrating different urban scales, the project develops a village spirit that recalls old Saint-Pierre.

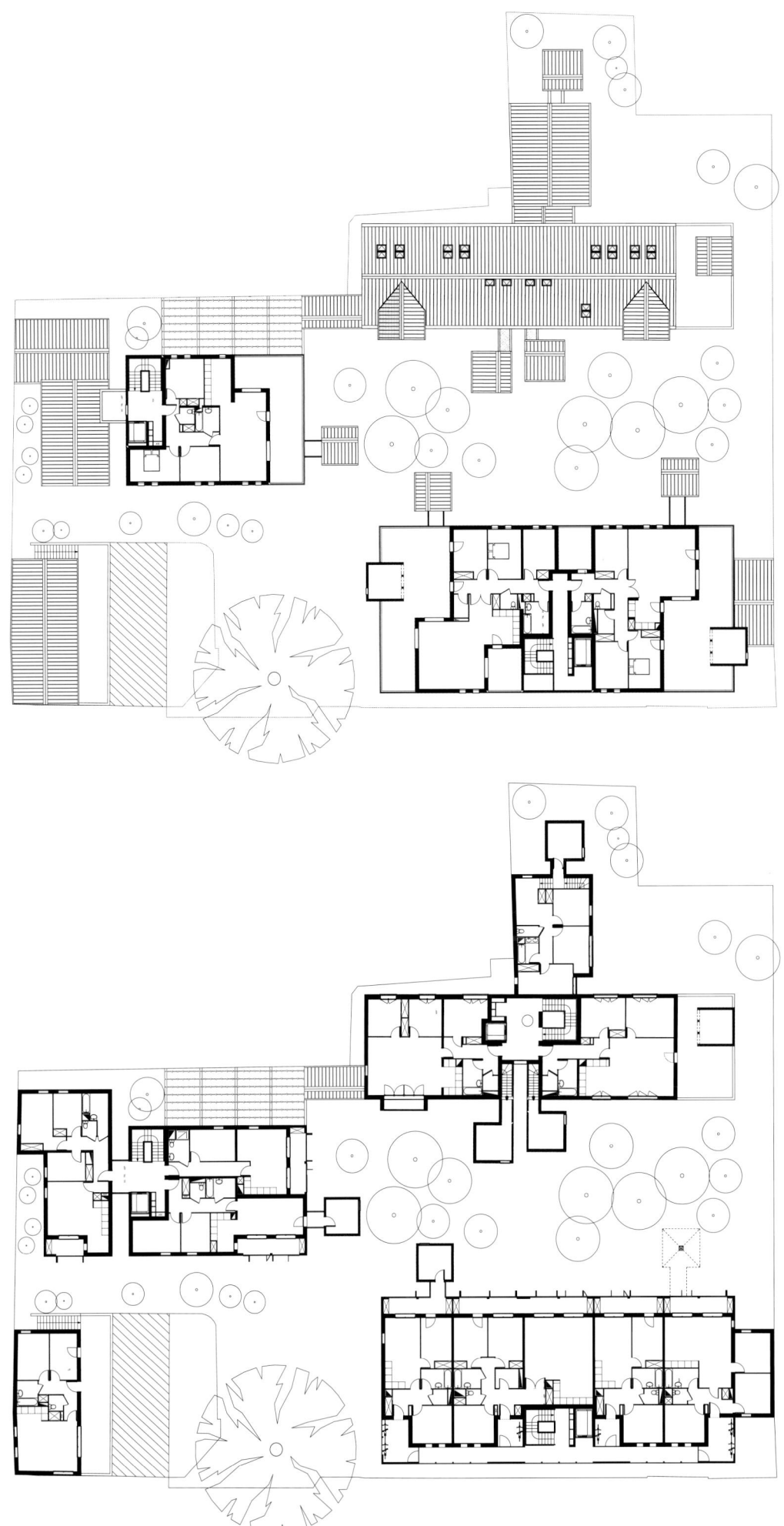

1, 2. Elevations.
3. Attic and roof plan.
4. Standard-floor plan.

ST/CTM urban development, Chambray-lès-Tours, Indre-et-Loire, 2017, unrealized competition entry

The response to a competition launched in 2017 by the borough of Chambray-lès-Tours, this project concerned the development of a large urban block on a future avenue that is scheduled to welcome a tram line. Comprising a diversity of uses (housing and business accommodation), the programme stipulated different dwelling typologies to encourage a social and generational mix. Even if Barrier's proposal did not win, it allowed him to experiment with new approaches and was the occasion for a research project undertaken by his office: the design of an entire ecological neighbourhood.

A city-scale room comprising three buildings grouped around a garden, the project creates an urban front that matches the scale of the future main avenue (the Avenue de la République) while ensuring a transition between the business and residential buildings. A composition of unequal volumes accompanies the site's topography, cadencing this part of the avenue. Through their disposition in an open U, the different structures create openings and views between the avenue and the heart of the block.

The porosity and permeability between the urban space and the interior garden are prolonged via a network of pathways and soft-transport links that connect the ensemble to Chambray-lès-Tours's various sites and facilities. Though all the dwellings are directly accessed from the street or the garden, the fluidity of space from the interior towards the exterior is preserved. This open space at the heart of the urban block is not only a green backdrop but also allows cultivation of produce (permaculture), while its greenery ensures the continuity of the existing link between green and blue networks. Plants crown the roofs of all three buildings thanks to the presence of maisonettes with gardens on the final floors. This ecological approach also comprises wind turbines to supply electricity for the communal areas and a reservoir near the shared kitchen gardens to supply some of the water requirements.

Barrier invented a whole architectural language for this ecological approach, guided by the fact that the buildings need to adapt to seasonal variations: all the dwellings feature through accommodation (north–south or east–west), with façades comprising several layers that both insulate and filter sunlight, thereby providing improved comfort in both winter and summer. The shutters-loggia-balcony sequence (on the courtyard) forms a succession of strata that are complemented by outdoor walkways (most of which are oriented towards the street side) that, as well as accessing the dwellings, create a permanent random effect that dematerializes the external envelope of these three buildings. The traditional wall thus dissolves into a succession of layers.

This impression is made possible by the implementation of a rational architectural and structural system comprising a lightweight wooden frame for the different façade strata, steel for the articulations and hand rails, and pre-lacquered zinc for the gently sloping roofs. The dominance of a mono-materiality (wood) creates an effect of homogeneity, despite the internal complexity. This is a generous approach in which ecology is not just a technical question but one that transforms these layered façades into convivial spaces of encounter via the walkways, as well as reinforcing the idea that the balcony is a room in its own right.

Almost the entire envelope on the courtyard side features folding in timber, which, besides insulating from heat and cold, offers the dwellings extra living space.

1. General plan with standard floor.
2. Computer drawing seen from the Avenue de la République.
3. Computer drawing of the interior garden.

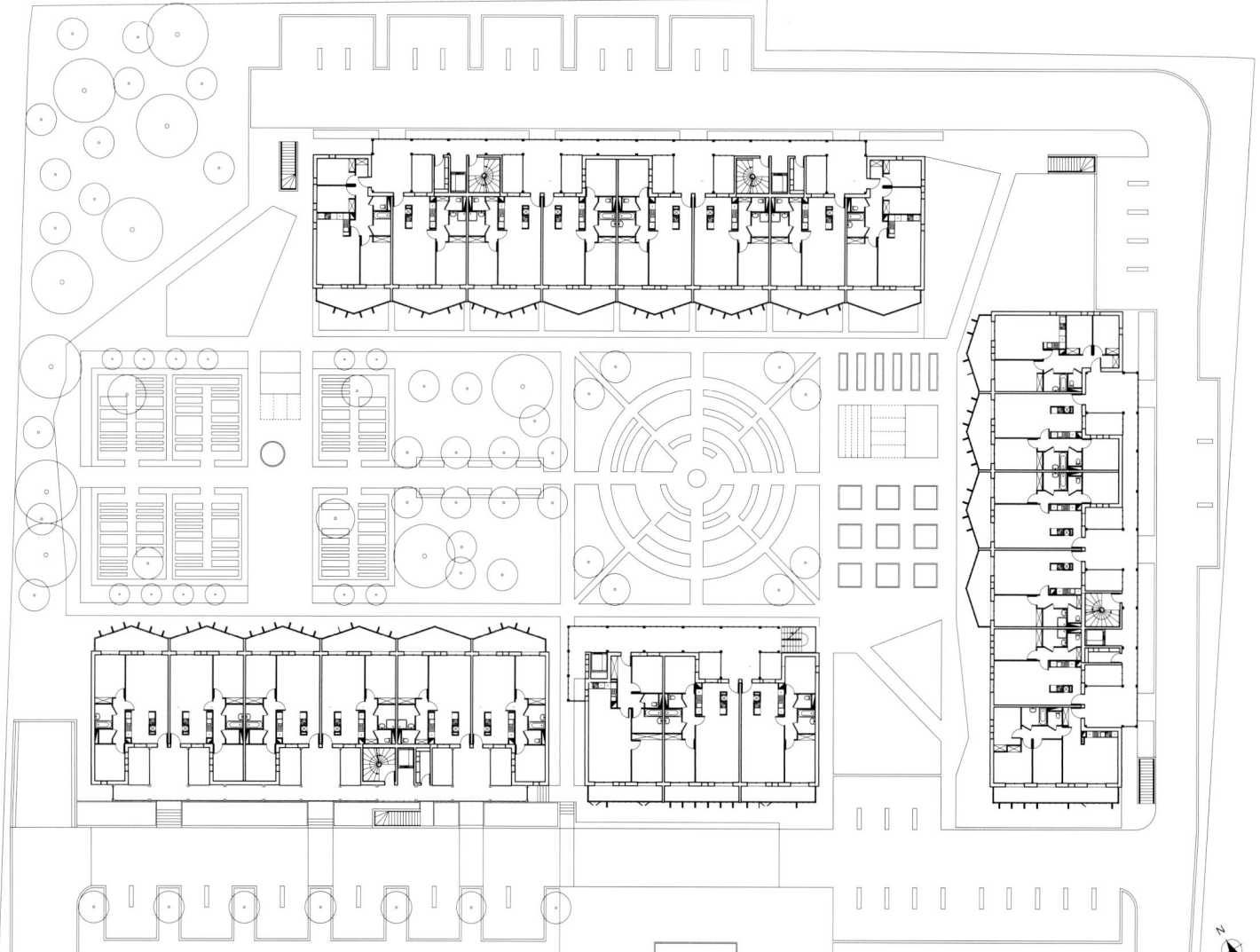

Experiments with houses

Though houses are but a small part of Barrier's practice, they form a laboratory in which he can explore innovations that will benefit other projects to come. In particular, they were the opportunity to experiment with bioclimatic and domotic design, such as his pioneering 1990 domotic house in Chambray-lès-Tours, which afterwards informed the 1994 Résidence du Mai in Chinon, a housing scheme for the disabled where some of the technical equipment can be controlled remotely from beds and wheelchairs. Here, three very different houses are discussed: the transformation of the Paumelle House in 2006–09 and of the Villa Serge in 2008–12, and the 2017 unbuilt ULUL House, an all-timber project submitted for a competition organized by the Domaine de la Bourdaisière.

Realized for Yvonne and Philippe Paumelle, owners of the Oniris art gallery in Rennes, the first of the three concerns a 1970s regionalist-style granite house in Brittany, which Barrier transformed into a more contemporary, fluid home that is better adapted to its owners' artistic penchants. As well as entirely reconfiguring the room layout around a large living area, he altered fenestration and doorways to open up interior perspectives that continue outside, via a large terrace and a small patio, into a sculpture park and an aromatic garden. To create a connection with the outdoor landscape and transform the rather compact dwelling into something freer, Barrier added two glass volumes: a cubic winter garden that prolongs the dining room, and a small freestanding vertical greenhouse between the terrace and the patio. Large glazed bays replaced the old French doors with their small panes, harmonizing with the simplicity of the metal-grid structures of the greenhouse additions. This desire to unify the new and old parts of the house can also be found in the treatment of the interior space, which has become an enfilade of »white cubes«, a sort of extension of Oniris inside the home, where works by François Morellet, Claude Viallat, Vera Molnár and others are displayed. In this way, the owners' professional and personal lives become one in their private home.

The Villa Serge is Barrier's own house on the Île d'Yeu (Vendée). Built around 1906, it was one of the first of its kind on the island and is the archetype of the seaside home, with its front garden whose wall is cadenced by terracotta urns, its ironwork, and its park surrounded by a high stone enclosure and planted with exotic species. Originally square in plan, the house had been extended over the years to the rear, with little coherence among the various parts. Barrier chose to work with what he had by inverting the functions, creating a central »street« that accesses all parts of the house; in this way, he created a perspective that traverses the entire dwelling and its history, and opens onto the park. As a result, the interior is divided up symmetrically, but where the day spaces with their large windows were formerly oriented north, towards the sea, the house now opens towards the south, onto a large terrace and the garden. As in the Paumelle House, the new rooms are treated as white cubes to provide a suitable backdrop for the owners' art collection, while the old part of the building, with its panelling and tiled flooring, has been restored in the spirit of the origi-

nal. The more minimalist approach adopted in the remodelling of the extensions transforms these spaces to adapt them to a new lifestyle: the central street accesses on one side the sitting room, which doubles up as a gallery for Post-Impressionist Île d'Yeu painters (Bertrand, Lecomte, Callot, Murique, Dezaunay, Nassivet, as well as the leader of the Saint-Jean-de-Monts school, Eugène Corneau), and on the other the dining room, which showcases contemporary pieces by Vera Molnár, Aurélie Nemours, Morellet, Viallat, Bonnefoi and others. The street itself, which is top-lit, serves as an exhibition space for the new generation of painters working on the Île d'Yeu.

While the two houses discussed above were experiments in the transformation and rehabilitation of existing regionalist and seaside properties, the third (unrealized) example was an experiment in eco-living, the result of Barrier's participation in the first edition of the Festival of Woods and Forests at the Domaine de la Bourdaisière in Montlouis-sur-Loire. Held in 2016, the event brought together a wide public as well as the main players in the French timber industry, the festival's goal being to help make France a leader in timber construction and biosourced materials. Under the competition rules, the ULUL House, as Barrier named it, had to be constructed entirely in wood or timber-derived materials, including all the interior fittings: sanitary equipment, textiles, insulation, energy production, the roof, all the furniture, the kitchen, the heating, the plumbing, the wall coverings, the foundations, etc. There was also a requirement to favour local materials, in particular species available from La Bourdaisière: sequoia, cedar, hazel, oak, acacia, sycamore and box. Intended as a prototype contemporary dwelling, the all-timber house was required to have a floor surface of at least 36 m² on two levels, be capable of disassembly and transport to other sites, and cost no more than 150,000, a sum that had to cover everything, from initial studies to construction.

Barrier proposed a project that demonstrated all the requirements set forth in the brief in an easily readable way. Measuring 85 m², the ULUL House uses different types of wood and timber derivatives (wood wool, pulp, cellulose, etc.), with bamboo for the plumbing and the wind-turbine mast, wicker for the light fittings, and fruit-tree timber for the furniture. Formally, the house adopts the soft organic curves found in plant life, using a strong, simple structure: a pointed arch, like an upturned ship, which brings all the loads down to the ground and creates a free, spacious and elegant internal volume. In the manner of a Quonset Hut, the roof descends to grade, minimizing construction time and the amount of materials used, while digital prefabrication ensures rapid manufacture. The fluid, vaulted form, of which one part is raised to form the second level, imprints its character on the interior, as though everything were carved from a single timber block: the dining table rises seamlessly from the floorboards, which also become benches, while closets, bookcases, and shelving are fully integrated into this formal and material unity. By combining nature and innovation with structural experimentation and a formal language that conceptualizes the architecture within the parameters of sustainable development, the ULUL House advances the ecological approach in house building.

1. Paumelle House. Plan.
2. Paumelle House. The sculpture garden.

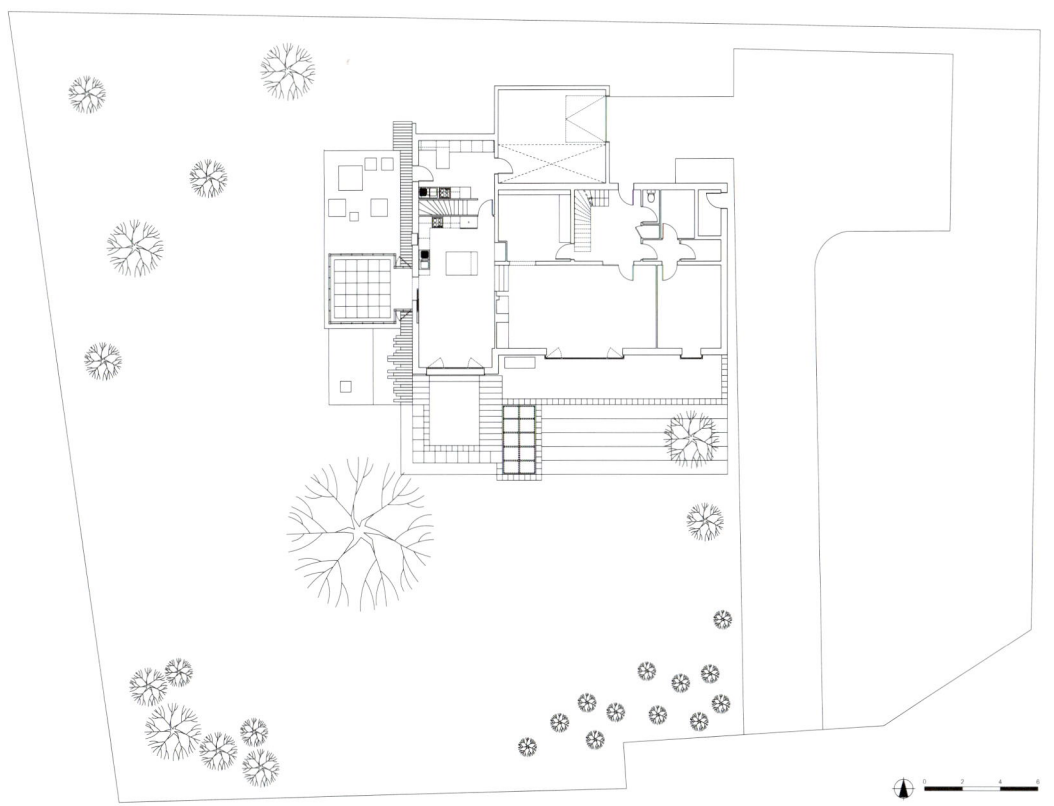

3. Paumelle House. The winter garden.
4. Paumelle House. The small greenhouse.

5. Villa Serge. Ground-floor plan.
6. Villa Serge. The garden.
7. Villa Serge. The small patio.

8. Villa Serge. The painter's salon.
9. Villa Serge. The studio.

ULUL
Nature & innovation
JYB MAISON 100%BOIS

La maison **ŬLUL** est inspirée des formes végétales souples, des courbes organiques que l'on trouve dans le monde végétal. Sa structure est simple, résistante, efficace : un arc brisé comme un bateau ou une chaînette renversée qui ramène au sol toutes les forces de compression en libérant un espace intérieur libre, spacieux, élégant.

Le désir d'utiliser la géométrie de la nature n'est pas nouveau dans l'architecture mais se traduit rarement dans l'habitat.

L'évolution des techniques de construction en ossature bois et notamment les nouvelles possibilités offertes par la découpe numérique de panneaux nous offre une liberté de conception oubliant l'empilement classique des matériaux pour concevoir des structures plus légères, des ensembles autoportants, préfabriqués en atelier et assemblés.

Déclinaisons possibles

Maison Type 2   Maison Type 3   Maison Type 4   Maison Type 3 avec pièce supplémentaire (atelier, garage, studio...)   Maison Type 3 avec pièce supplémentaire (atelier, garage, studio...) et serre ou pergola

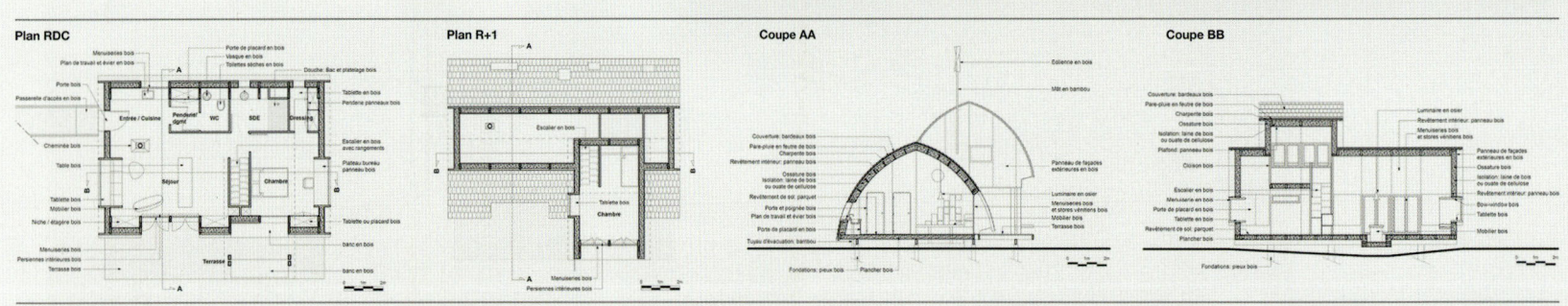

Plan RDC — Plan R+1 — Coupe AA — Coupe BB

Surfaces

Niveau RDC	
Entrée/Séjour/Cuisine	32,74 m²
Chambre + dressing	16,47 m²
Dégagement	2,23 m²
WC	2,22 m²
SDE	4,56 m²
Niveau R+1	
Chambre	11,90 m²
TOTAL	**70,12 m²**

Hors rangements et autres espaces sous la limite de hauteur des 1,80m

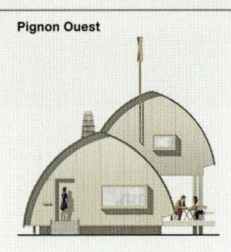

Pignon Ouest

Façade Nord

Façade Sud

Plan de masse

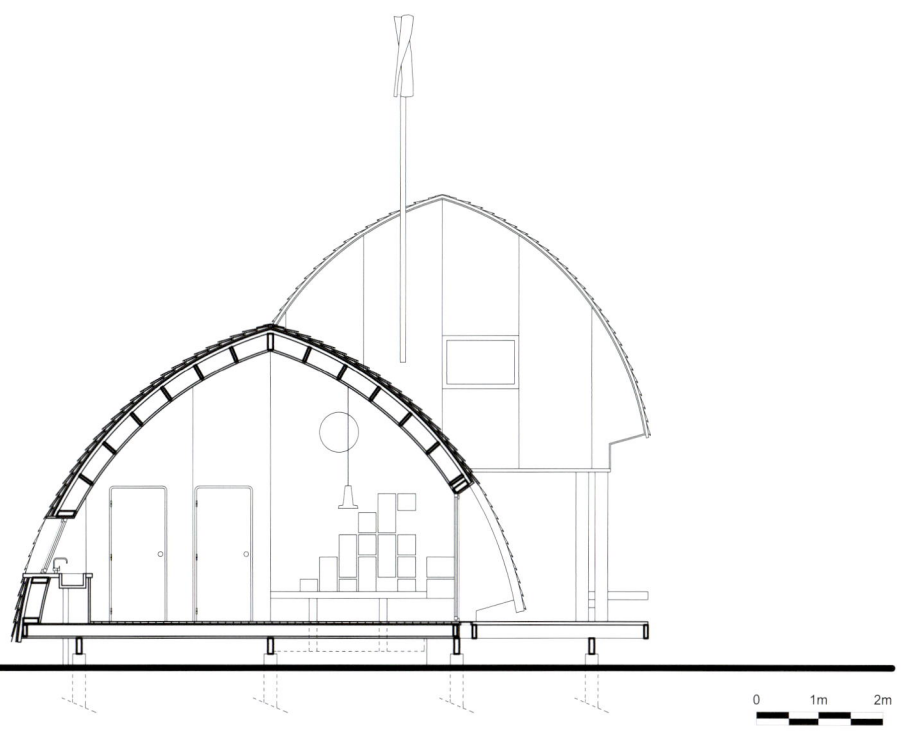

ULUL

Nature & innovation

Tout en bois, tout en soi : réinventer sa maison

Bien vivre c'est se sentir chez soi en tout lieu

et en particulier dans sa propre peau !

Il faudrait que toutes les maisons nous acceptent comme on est : des êtres en perpétuel mouvement entre le dedans et le dehors.

Une maison comme ça est forcément en bois, où l'on se sent dans un arbre, entre ciel et terre, entre rêves et désirs.

Les parfums de sève, la fraîcheur des feuillages, les variations de lumières attisent notre créativité. L'écorce respire, berce, applaudit à la pluie, se love dans le vent, invente le confort suprême d'être bien à l'abri par tous les temps.

La maison ŬLUL préserve intacte sa nature végétale

Elle évolue de façon organique, transformable à la manière d'une greffe arboricole. On devient jardinier de son espace à vivre, on peut faire croître les volumes, sans rien bouleverser de l'esprit initial.

La vigueur cylindrique des troncs est bien présente, un système constructif autonome rend les arcs pleinement habitables, pas d'armature encombrante, la coque du bateau qu'on inverse est une large pirogue.

Chaque découpe dessine des formes d'art, aussi fines que de la haute couture, aussi profilées que des fuselages : une plante est belle parce que les mille détails qui la cisèlent génèrent chacun à sa place l'esthétique achevée de l'ensemble.

« Le temps est le plus grand innovateur »[1]

Les forêts multi centenaires n'ont cessé de montrer combien le bois vit et résiste sereinement : le défi aujourd'hui est de lui rendre justice, longtemps délaissé mais toujours disposé à construire nos maisons à 100%.

[1] Francis Bacon, philosophe anglais, Essais (1625)

Ambiance intérieure de la salle de séjour et du coin repas/bibliothèque déclinant l'utilisation du bois et ses dérivés pour les objets du quotidien et la décoration : mobiliers, stores, assises, tapis, vaisselle, luminaires, jeux, sculptures en bois de récupération...

Auberge de jeunesse de Tours, Tours, Indre-et-Loire, 2016–19

Located on the Avenue de Grammont in the heart of Tours, this youth hostel creates a new urban landmark in the city. Part of an 8,500 m² development on the site of the now-demolished Sainte-Marguerite buildings, it offers 1,800 m² of floor space on eight levels, with 116 beds divided up among 45 rooms and a family suite, as well as a restaurant, a bar and reception areas. Barrier was asked to design everything both inside and out, including furniture and the night-time lighting of the façade.

Architecturally, the new youth hostel takes its cue from the surrounding heritage, though it can be read on several levels. At first glance it seems to integrate into this section of the Avenue de Grammont by imitating a grand 18th-century town house, respecting the cornice lines and tripartite façade divisions (base, main floors, attic) of the neighbouring classical buildings. However, a more detailed reading of the façade reveals that there is in fact nothing classical about its organization, since there is no plinth to lift the building away from the ground and no detailing or orthogonal organization of the fenestration in such a way as to structure the elevation. The apparently »random« play of windows is the result of the internal layout, for, unlike a hotel, the rooms are not all the same

but differ in size and shape (family suites, meeting rooms, bedrooms for two or four people), which is what generates the external appearance. This dynamic formal diversity also expresses in a more metaphorical sense the mix of different populations and nationalities that will use this hostel.

A third way of reading the façade can be found in its detailing. What might at first appear decorative, like the perforated laser-cut window and balcony railings, in fact takes its cue from the graphic quality and abstract design of the elevation. Distributed randomly, these features create a sense of dynamic, frenetic movement, with a similar effect on the courtyard façade. Like a musical score, a rhythmical vibration animates these two elevations, and helps dematerialize the building despite its mono-materiality (Richemont ashlar) and its monolithic aspect, a result of the very precise fitting together of three different sizes of stone block to produce a smooth surface. While this rhythmic vibration diminishes the façade's mass during the day, at night specially designed LED lighting (integrated into the railings) transforms it into a sparkling box.

Meanwhile, transparency and permeability also characterize the relationship between the street and the rear, since the large, glazed ground-floor bays allow views through to the garden, in such a way that the façade is no longer a wall that separates but an interface between outside and in that

allows the city to be seen in its physical depth. This coherence, which creates a continuity between the city and its architecture, is also found inside the building. Each space (reception, restaurant, corridors, bedrooms, etc.) enjoys its own specific design expressed through bespoke furnishings, lighting, textures and colours. To ensure each guest enjoys privacy in the bedrooms, which measure between 10 and 20 m² and accommodate up to four people, the bunk beds have been designed as little personal cabins, whose graphic quality corresponds to the high-design nature of the whole building, which extends even to the bike racks in the courtyard.

While specially designed furnishings characterize the bedrooms, the public areas (reception, restaurant and corridors) play on texture, materials and light. Looking to promote local craft, in particular wicker, Barrier commissioned the basketry cooperative in Villaines-les-Rochers (Indre-et-Loire) to make all the light shades and wall and ceiling coverings, so that the lightness of wicker dialogues with the compact mass of oak, which he specified for the tables at reception and in the restaurant (also made by a local firm). Completed by a specific chromatic light range diffused through bespoke fittings, the hostel's interior spaces flow fluidly into each other in such a way that the building's narrowness is entirely forgotten.

1. Main façade facing the Avenue de Grammont.
2. Garden-floor plan.
3. Ground-floor plan.
4. First-floor plan.
5. Second-floor plan.

pp. 118, 119
6. Main façade facing the Avenue de Grammont.
7. Rear façade facing the garden.

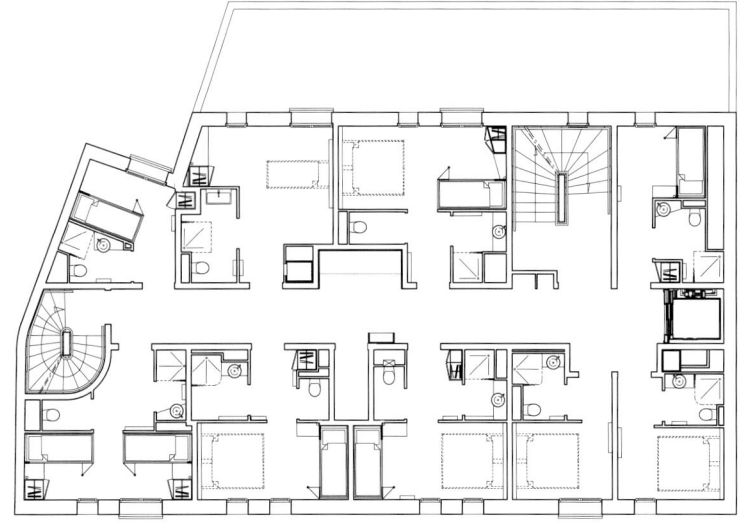

NIVEAU R+2

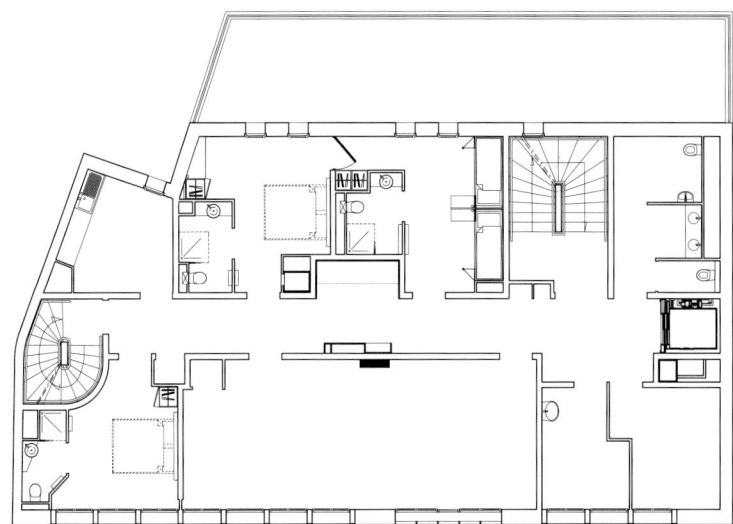

NIVEAU R+1

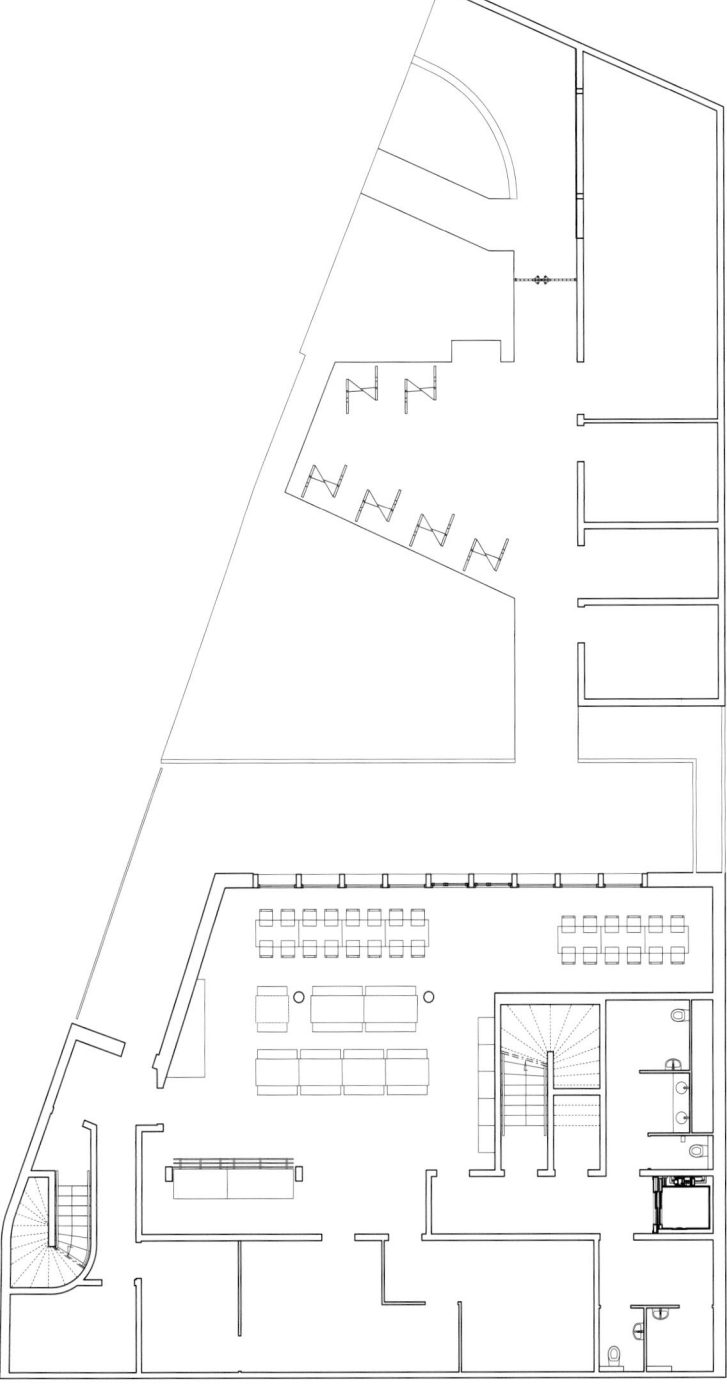

NIVEAU REZ-DE-JARDIN

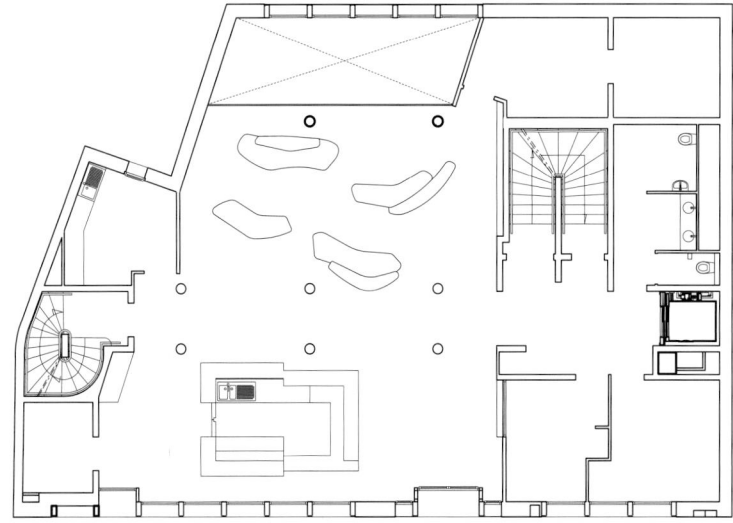

NIVEAU RDC

8. The restaurant on the garden floor.
9. The bar in the entrance hall on the ground floor.

10. Bedroom corridor.
11. Four-bed room.
12. Double-bed room.

Les Coqueplicots, Carrefour de l'Hippodrome, Chambray-lès-Tours, Indre-et-Loire, 2015–17

Located at the southern entrance to Chambray-lès-Tours, in the heart of the avenue Grand-Sud shopping area, the Carrefour de l'Hippodrome first received Barrier's attention back in 1989, when, with the lighting designer Pierre Rideau, he created a light installation made up of 32 methacrylate columns. Hailed internationally for its technical and aesthetic excellence, the installation was deemed too energy hungry 23 years later, leading the municipality to launch a modernization programme in 2012.

Barrier's new project takes its cue from the columns' grid layout, and once again uses light to mark the entrance to the borough with a strong installation that, as well as highlighting this major traffic axis, creates a symbolic perspective and an instantly recognisable landmark. The name he gave it, the *Coqueplicots*, is a deformation of the French word *coquelicot* – poppy – with the letter P added to include the word *pli*, or fold. This is a reference to a recurrent approach in Barrier's œuvre in which the fold becomes a fundamental part of his plastic and architectural language, as can be seen in his sculptures and design objects, as well as in many of the façades of his buildings.

The replacement installation features 552 *Coqueplicots*, each one comprising a folded and inclined red fluorescent Altuglas disc perched 3 to 4 m from the ground on a semi-rigid »stalk«, so that they bend gently with the wind. Deploying a strict geometric form and a strong primary colour, the result, through a game of multiplication, creates a work whose presence is astonishingly intense, by both day and night. Thanks to the use of LEDs, the new installation consumes seven times less electricity than the old, and features planting that includes lavender and blue fescue to unify the space circumscribed by the roundabout.

In its rather humdrum edge-of-town surroundings, the *Coqueplicots* makes a strong impact, particularly in the way it creates a coloured line when seen from afar, a focal point on the horizon. Moving closer, perception of the work changes as the installation reveals itself to be both dynamic and kinetic, located somewhere on the frontier between land and public art.

»Poppies have progressively disappeared from the countryside with the use of pesticides«, says Barrier, »but they used to be a common roadside wildflower. They were a great inspiration to the Impressionists, those painters of light, such as Claude Monet.« More than a mere roundabout decoration, then, the *Coqueplicots* are an artwork unto itself.

1. From afar a coloured line on the horizon of the traffic axis.
2, 3. Plan and elevation.

pp. 126/127
4. As the roundabout approaches, the *Coqueplicots* fly away like »a swarm of butterflies«.

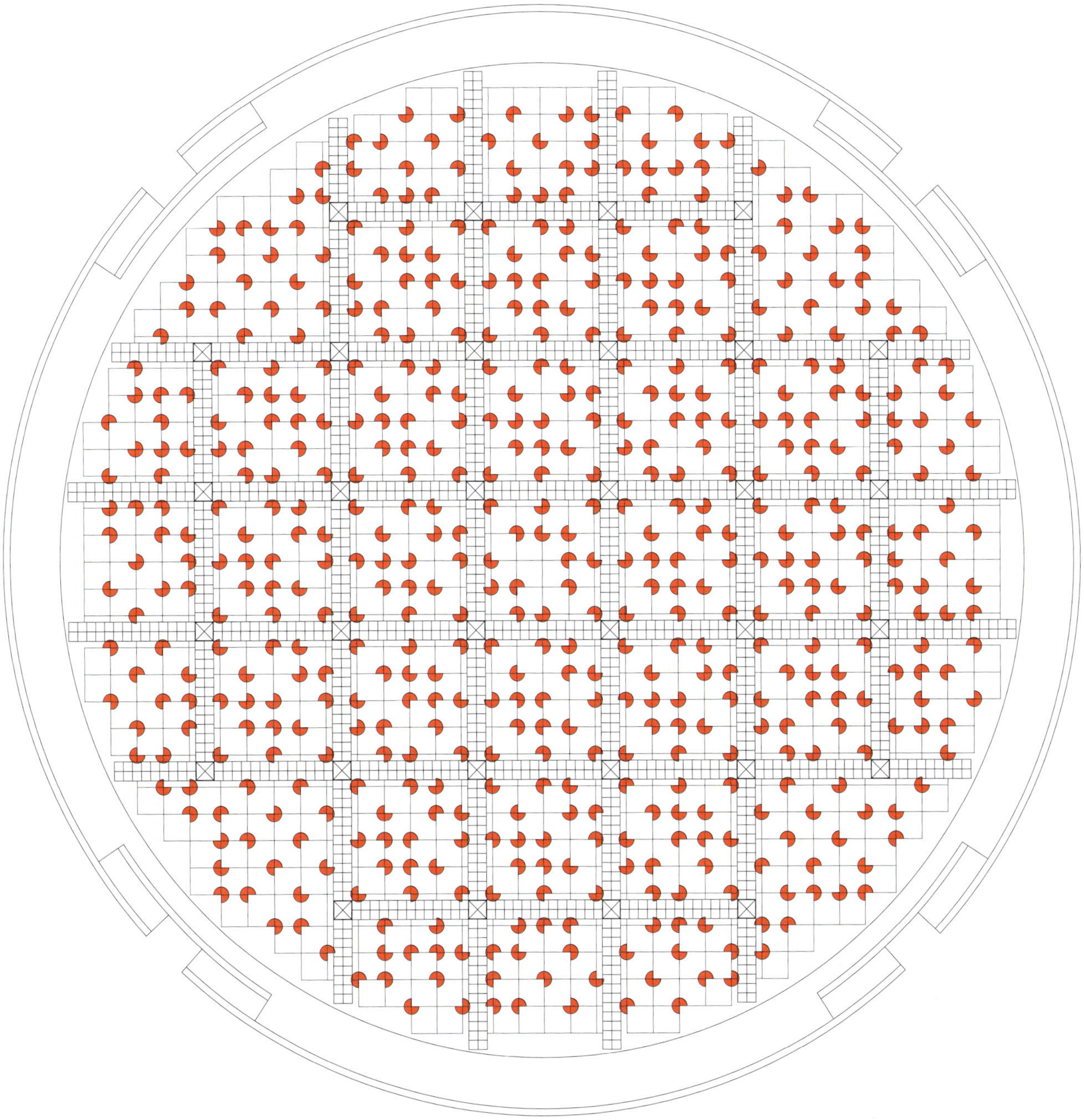

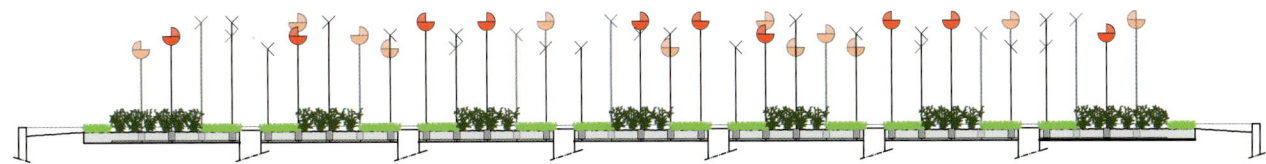

Furniture and design objects

According to the International Council of Societies of Industrial Design (ICSID), the discipline is »a creative activity that seeks to determine the formal properties of industrially produced objects. This includes their external characteristics but principally the structural and functional relationships that bring coherence to an object, both from the manufacturer's and the user's point of view.« Barrier, who has been producing objects, furniture, and interiors since 2009, has a rather different understanding of what design means, closer to the German *Gestaltung*, a difficult-to-translate term that refers to a global process of creation from initial conception to formal development and fabrication. »Design«, in the Barrier sense, is thus an artistic process that results in often unique, handmade pieces, with frequent recourse to innovative techniques (digital laser cutting) in the handling of materials such as wood, glass, metal and wicker, and a constant search for balance between form and function.

Barrier considers function in two phases. First, he develops a final form that is based both in the use of regulating lines (which, as we have seen, he often employs in his architecture) and in the physcial properties of the materials and manufacturing processes selected. This methodical approach allows variations of each object to be produced, since they are all derivations of a form that relates to a universal matrix. Barrier's folded, rectangular, rounded, curved, or organic pieces feature either smooth finishes (sometimes matte, sometimes shiny) or textured surfaces that are the product of the natural structure of the material (wicker, ribbed aluminium, etc.). Then, in a second phase, Barrier seeks to »enhance« and »exalt« the function, producing a specific language through analogical transposition. A graphic and plastic vocabulary, associated either with a chromatic range or with black and white, produces an image of functionality that offers a pared-down, minimalist simplicity. The resulting objects stand out in their exactitude and timelessness.

Barrier's approach is in some ways comparable to the U.S. Maker movement, which emerged in the early 2000s in reaction to industrialization. Adopting a DIY approach to manufacture, Makers use innovative technology to create prototypes and pay particular attention to learning new practical skills, which are then creatively applied in a local context. In the same way, Barrier seeks out craftspeople, manufacturers, and industrialists (both local and regional) who are willing to develop the final product with him. Such collaborations are also born of a desire to favour local, circular production, thereby reducing the carbon footprint of the objects in question, which are often made in a single location. But these currents in contemporary design are just one reference in Barrier's approach, since he also looks back to the French scene of the 1950s, which was characterized by structural ingenuity, a technique of assemblage and variations, and the possibility of serial manufacture starting from prototypes.

Seeking to reinvent the typologies of traditional furniture in order to adapt them to the size and proportions of contemporary dwellings, Barrier began producing design collections in 2009, but already in the early 1990s was making one-off pieces for private and public clients such as the municipal library in Saint-Pierre-des-Corps (1988 to 1992), the Paumelle House and contemporary art gallery in Rennes (2003/04). Moreover, it was on the latter commission that he met and began working with the artisans of the »furniture road« (between Rennes and Saint-Malo), which gave him the idea of developing design series.

In 2009, he founded JYB Édition in order to produce his own range of furniture and accessories, and a year later showed his very first collection, *Et si c'était une belle journée* (*And If It Were a Beautiful Day*), in Paris, Nantes, and Tours. Comprising several models in lacquered MDF, some of which sport finely ribbed aluminium façades, the collection includes a cocktail cabinet, a small credenza (with and without a bench prolongation), a storage unit with diagonally mounted doors, and the Éclipse coffee table. The strength of the collection's concept is to be found in its great simplicity of composition – a main body sandwiched between two planks and raised up on legs –, while variations allow for different use typologies, expressed through both proportions and the inclusion of fold-down flaps, niches, drawers, the number of modules lined up together, etc. While the empty planks at either end prolong the different storage pieces in space, the black and white Éclipse comprises two circular table tops mounted on five legs, with the taller top pivoting around the shorter.

Also present in this collection, halfway between sculpture and object, is the Tol'Pli modular shelving system in folded, lacquered sheet steel. Offering a wide range of different assembly possibilities, Tol'Pli forms a decorative architectural composition in which colours are freely associated within a logic of geometry. As for the Tol'Rigami lamp, realized and co-produced in sheet steel with Confidence and Light, its multiple folds form an all-in-one base-cum-shade whose form expresses ideas of both light and stability. Two formats are available: a 41.2 cm-high table lamp and a 180 cm-high standard lamp, the latter offering both direct and indirect lighting.

In 2014, at YaMaKaDo in Paris, Barrier launched his Bi'Pli range, a new type of modular storage that is sold in parts which are easy to transport and assemble. The ingenious constructive system comprises folded sheet-steel bookends that hook into notches in the planks: once fixed onto the plinth, they allow the creation of free-standing bookshelves whose length is adaptable according to use, and whose height is simply the product of the number of bookends superimposed.

While Barrier's early pieces combined wood and metal, his 2020 »Chant de Verre« collection, realized for the »Maison & Objet« furniture fair, combined glass and metal to produce a series of lamps and vases. Among the pieces are a 50 cm-high lamp, a 38 cm-tall vase, as well as a smaller vase integrated into a Tol'Pli to form a wall console, all realized thanks to the engineering skills of Verart, a French company specialized (among others) in blowtorch-finished blown-glass objects and lights. Not only did Barrier widen Verart's range with these unique handmade crystal pieces, he also proposed a new technical combination: manufactured without a mould, and placed on a round, flat lacquered-metal base, three cylindrical forms that get smaller in size towards the top are superimposed. Blowtorch finishing allows such a degree of perfection that the transition between the three cylinders is entirely invisible, making these objects appear as though frozen in a fluid movement. One can't help but make the comparison with the Bauhaus artist and designer Wilhelm Wagenfeld (1900–1990), whose extremely light and fine glass objects were described as having been »sculpted in air«.

1–6. Study sketches.

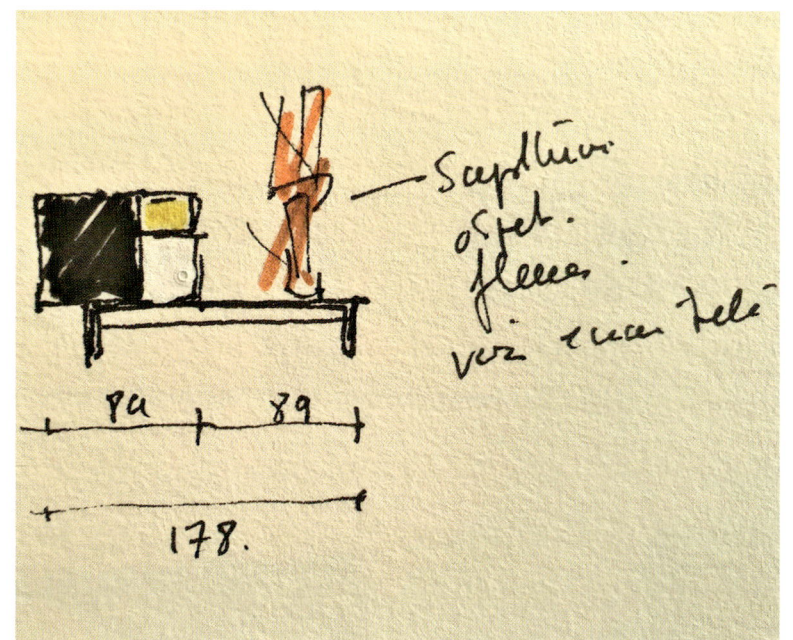

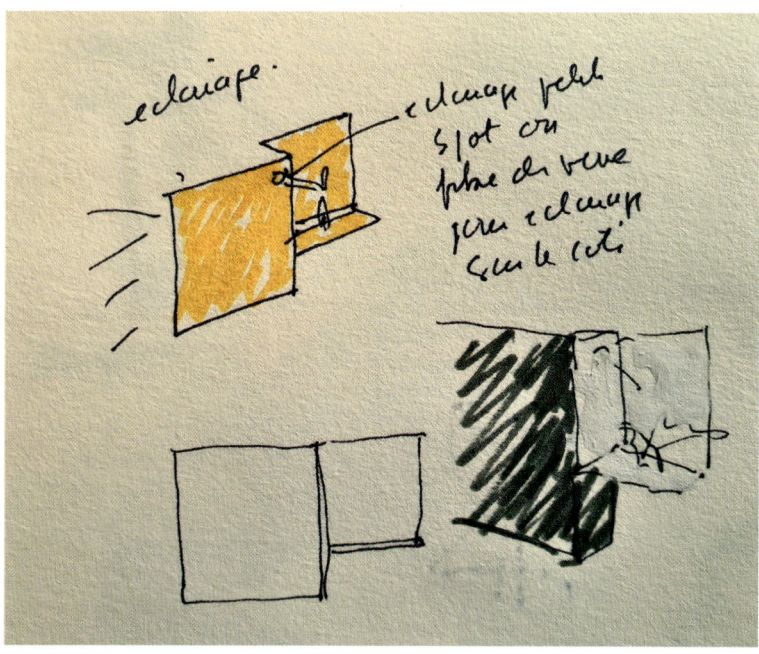

Art installations in Audilab headquarters, Saint-Pierre-des-Corps, Indre-et-Loire, 2017–21

Since 2014, Barrier has been modelling the urban composition of the new neighbourhood around the TGV station in Saint-Pierre-des-Corps, where he built the Cap 55 complex comprising three buildings constructed in several phases (see page 36). In 2017, after the hearing-aid specialist Audilab acquired four floors in the second building, the company's founder and director, Benoît Roy, decided to link the two final levels with a monumental staircase that leads to a roof terrace with sweeping views across the river of rail tracks.

Though the stairway was lit and dramatized thanks to the introduction of a huge bay of façade glazing, Roy still wasn't satisfied, and sought to make it even more attractive. After abandoning the idea of bringing in flowering plants, he asked Barrier, who had just completed the *Coquelicots* at the Carrefour de l'Hippodrome in Chambray-lès-Tours (see page 126), to come up with a proposal for the whole stairway. In this way, rather than the mere recipient of an artwork, the staircase would become an artwork unto itself. Barrier was immediately accepted by Roy.

His intervention features seven identical pieces that are suspended at different heights in the staircase, their folded-disc form directly recalling the *Coquelicots*. For the colours, on the other hand, he took his cue from the building's façade and used black and white. Each piece is realized in painted sheet steel with a radius of 60 cm (120 cm diameter). As visitors move up and down the stairs, they perceive the changing relationship between the pieces, discovering them from different angles and observing the play of light and shadow. Lightweight enough to move in the breeze, the pieces dance an aerial ballet as they follow the curve of the stair.

I

n a figurative sense, each piece recalls a hand cupped around the ear in order to hear better, evoking, as the visitor ascends, words caught in mid flight. Moreover, as Barrier explains, the installation's title, *7 sur 7*, also pays tribute to the man who commissioned it. »Benoît Roy works every day of the week – *7 jours sur 7* – while in French we also have the expression ›*je vous reçois 5 sur 5*‹, which means ›I hear you loud and clear‹. So Roy hears us seven out of seven.« Though both the glazed bay and the stair are an integral part of the architecture, they also have a formal existence in their own right, constituting a global visual feature that establishes a relationship between the interior and the exterior. By allowing daylight in and artificial light out, the ensemble plays the role of a luminous sign as well as constituting a display case for the art installation.

Though it is fairly unusual to design both a building and the artwork within it, this approach is emblematic of Barrier's conception of architecture, his being a transversal method in which the artwork becomes an integral part of the building and vice versa.

In 2021, Roy commissioned a second art installation for another staircase that, though less monumental, links every floor in the office. Barrier's intervention consists in a 14.5 m-high and 3 m-wide fresco whose design accompanies the rise of the stair, its amorphous forms in black, white, and blue (the colour of Audilab) producing a curved pattern that climbs with and mirrors the spiral of the steps. Developed from a small sketch, which itself was inspired by a decorative detail in a piece of wallpaper, the fresco motif has been blown up 300 times to reach a degree of abstraction at the scale of the staircase. At night, theatre lighting dramatizes the work, which, like 7/7, is visible from outside through a large glazed bay.

1–3. The amorphous shapes accompanying the spiral staircase.
4. Detailed view of the pieces.

pp. 138, 139
5, 6. The installation on the grand staircase.

Nomad sculptures, 2015

With design objects like the *Tol'Pli* shelves, the *Tol'rigami* lamp, and the *Bi'Pli* storage units, Barrier has been experimenting with techniques of folding and laser cutting since 2008. For almost ten years now, he has also been channelling this research into sculptures, producing work located at the interface between art and architecture. While sculpture had already conquered the public realm in his œuvre, particularly with his light columns at the Carrefour de l'Hippodrome in Chambray-lès-Tours (which he transformed in 2017 into the installation the *Coqueplicots*, he has since widened his sculptural practice to include other scales.

Barrier began a first series, titled *Nomades*, in 2014, of which the initial expression was a 36 x 36 x 58 cm cardboard model of five »possibles« or »infinitely combinable multiples« that expressed a synthesis of folding and asymmetrical cutting. To underline this investigation into planes, surfaces, and lines, Barrier applied colour – both primary (red, yellow, and blue) and complementary (green) – as well as black and white. Intending to transpose his design to a bigger scale and monumentalize it in metal, Barrier baptized it »nomad« in reference to the idea of »migration« between different scales, as well as, on a more practical level, to ease of transport, since the sculptures can be taken apart, forming a perfect square or rectangle once folded for packing.

The first *Nomad* was realized in 2015 in lacquered aluminium. Measuring 216 x 144 x 108 cm, it represents a technical exploit in the cutting and forming of three flat, dissymmetrical, independent yellow pieces that are combined with a white mobile part. The latter, a scalene triangle attached at one extremity, gently moves whenever there is a breeze. Thanks to a cut-out in the piece to which it is attached, the triangle can rotate 360° around its axis and, whenever it is perfectly aligned with its support, a geometrical figure reminiscent of a kite is created by the association of the triangle and its hollow »double«. Through this optical illusion, void becomes matter and, if only for an instant (depending on the strength and direction of the wind), what is usually perceived as dissymmetrical becomes a symmetrical geometrical object, achieving a momentary equilibrium in space.

If the ideas of a form suspended in equilibrium, of movement occurring through natural forces, of delimiting space through sculpture, of transforming void into matter, and of a sculpture that is at once static and mobile recall the work of the American artist Alexander Calder (1898–1976), it's no accident: Barrier got to know him in the early 1970s in his studio in Saché, near Tours, and later helped him with the installation of a stabile at Tours's Institut universitaire de technologie. Though the link to Calder may seem obvious, Barrier's conceptual method nonetheless finds its source in his work as an architect, because the *Nomades* were born from the use of regulating lines as well as from his experiments with folding and metal working. In this way, Barrier's *Nomadic* sculptures demonstrate how different disciplines – design, sculpture, architecture, composition, town planning – are intertwined in his œuvre, with everything always originating from the same design method.

1. Five models from the *Nomad* series.
2, 3. A large *Nomad* sculpture in the garden of the Villa Datris for the »Archi-Sculpture« exhibition in 2015.

Credits for the selected buildings and projects

Headquarters for the *Ouest France* editorial team, Île de Nantes, Nantes, Loire-Atlantique,
2006–08
Clients: *Ouest France*/Icade 3GA
Associate site manager: TRIADE Architectes
Sanitary and electrical consultant: Isocrate
Work coordination: Ouest Coordination

Blanc Carroi shopping centre, Chinon, Indre-et-Loire
2007–14
Clients: Soradis/La Plaine des Vaux
Associate site manager: Logic Ingénierie

Leclerc de Fondettes shopping centre, Fondettes, Indre-et-Loire
2015/16, project
Client: SAS Fondis

Orangery at the botanical garden in Tours, Indre-et-Loire
2006–09
Client: Ville de Tours, Service bâtiments
Technical and economic consultant: IMC 2
Structural engineering: Autec Ingénierie

Covered tennis courts in Vanves, Hauts-de-Seine
2003–06
Client: Ville de Vanves, Service des sports
Technical consultant: INGERCO

Cap 55, Saint-Pierre-des-Corps, Indre-et-Loire
2009–21
Clients: Sogeprom/Centre Immo Promotion
Technical consultant: IMC2

Urban elevator in Chinon, Indre-et-Loire
2006–08
Clients: Ville de Chinon /SET
Technical consultant: Iosis

Les Papeteries de Bretagne redevelopment, Rennes, Ille-et-Vilaine
2006–13
Client: SCCV Les Papeteries
Sanitary consultant: THALEM Ingénierie
Economic consultant, associate site manager: Nantes Exe

Résidence Carré Verde, Vertou, Loire-Atlantique
2009–13
Client: ICADE Promotion Logement
Technical consultants: Bet Callu, Nantes Exe

Résidence Les Brandons, Blainville-sur-Orne, Calvados
2000–07
Client: La Plaine Normande
Technical consultant: Ouest Coordination

La Guignardière eco-neighbourhood, Chambray-lès-Tours, Indre-et-Loire
2016–23
Client: Ville de Chambray-lès-Tours
External works engineer: Geoplus

Résidence Le Bois, Moult, Calvados
2010/11
Client: La Plaine Normande
Technical consultant: IMC2

Résidence Blériot, Tours, Indre-et-Loire
2011–15
Client: SCET
Technical consultants: IMC2/3iA

Résidence Cour Line Porcher, Saint-Pierre-des-Corps, Indre-et-Loire
2009–13
Clients: Cirmad Centre Sud Ouest/Val Touraine Habitat
Technical consultant: IMC2

Résidence Bonne Garde, Nantes, Loire-Atlantique
2008–14
Client: Nantes Habitat
Technical consultants: Bet Callu, Dupin, Nantes Exe

Jacques Decour development at the Monconseil eco-neighbourhood, Tours, Indre-et-Loire
2008–16
Clients: Tours Habitat/Touraine Logement
Technical consultants: IMC2/3iA

Résidence Les 3 rives, Rennes, Ille-et-Vilaine
2004–07
Client: Aiguillon Construction
Technical consultant: Thalem Ingéniérie

Zac Libera housing, Colombelles, Calvados
2010–14
Client: La Plaine Normande
Technical consultant: IMC2

Résidence Aquarelle, Chantepie, Ille-et-Vilaine
2006–08
Client: Coop Consruction
Technical consultant: IMC2

Résidence Le Cristalium, Tours, Indre-et-Loire
2012–15
Client: Tours Promotion
Technical consultant: IMC2

Résidence Les Jardins Boileau, Saint-Pierre-des-Corps, Indre-et-Loire
2010–13
Client: Nouveau Logis Centre Limousin
Technical consultant: IMC2

Résidence Canopée, Saint-Pierre-des-Corps, Indre-et-Loire
2020–
Client: Abscisse Promotion Résidentielle

ST/CTM urban development, Chambray-lès-Tours, Indre-et-Loire
2017, invited competition entry, project not selected
Client: Sogeprom
Technical consultant: Egis

Maison Paumelle, Betton, Ille-et-Vilaine
2006–09
Client: M. et Mme Paumelle

Villa Serge, Ile d'Yeu, Vendée
2008–12
Client: M. et Mme Barrier

Maison ULUL, La Bourdaisière, Indre-et-Loire
2017, study
Competition; favourite project of the public, not realized
Client: Louis Albert de Broglie

Auberge de jeunesse de Tours, Tours, Indre-et-Loire
2016–19
Client: 4e SET
Structural engineer, economic consultant: ABAC Ingénierie

Les Coqueplicots, Carrefour de l'Hippodrome, Chambray-lès-Tours, Indre-et-Loire
2015–17
Client: Ville de Chambray-lès-Tours
Lighting concept: LPLS

Agence Barrier   1981–2011
JYB Architecture   2011–
JYB Edition   2009–

Collaborators
Kim Pham   2001–2010
Frederic Sorel   2003–
Magali Chupeau   2004–2014
Amélie Fardeau   2007
Cyrielle Leval   2015–2016

Secretrary's office – administration
Sophie Barrier   1989–
Maryline Mauny   1996–2012
Melissa Lefebvre   2012–2018
Sandrine Girault   2013–2021